D1085208

616.2 Ser
Serradell, Joaquima
SARS /
$34.95   ocn429750088

5
8
2nd ed.   0

WITHDRAWN

DEADLY DISEASES AND EPIDEMICS

SARS

Second Edition

DEADLY DISEASES AND EPIDEMICS

Anthrax, Second Edition

Antibiotic-Resistant Bacteria

Avian Flu

Botulism

Campylobacteriosis

Cervical Cancer

Chicken Pox

Cholera, Second Edition

Dengue Fever and Other Hemorrhagic Viruses

Diphtheria

Ebola

Encephalitis

Escherichia coli Infections

Gonorrhea

Hantavirus Pulmonary Syndrome

Helicobacter pylori

Hepatitis

Herpes

HIV/AIDS

Infectious Diseases of the Mouth

Infectious Fungi

Influenza, Second Edition

Legionnaires' Disease

Leprosy

Lung Cancer

Lyme Disease

Mad Cow Disease

Malaria, Second Edition

Meningitis

Mononucleosis, Second Edition

Pelvic Inflammatory Disease

Plague, Second Edition

Polio, Second Edition

Prostate Cancer

Rabies

Rocky Mountain Spotted Fever

Rubella and Rubeola

Salmonella

SARS, Second Edition

Smallpox

Staphylococcus aureus Infections

Streptococcus (Group A)

Streptococcus (Group B)

Syphilis, Second Edition

Tetanus

Toxic Shock Syndrome

Trypanosomiasis

Tuberculosis

Tularemia

Typhoid Fever

West Nile Virus, Second Edition

Yellow Fever

DEADLY DISEASES AND EPIDEMICS

SARS

Second Edition

Joaquima Serradell, Ph.D., M.P.H.

CONSULTING EDITOR
Hilary Babcock, M.D., M.P.H.,
Infectious Diseases Division,
Washington University School of Medicine,
Medical Director of Occupational Health (Infectious Diseases),
Barnes-Jewish Hospital and St. Louis Children's Hospital

FOREWORD BY
David Heymann
World Health Organization

CHELSEA HOUSE
PUBLISHERS
An imprint of Infobase Publishing

SARS, Second Edition

Copyright © 2010 by Infobase Publishing

All rights reserved. No part of this book may be reproduced or utilized in any form or by any means, electronic or mechanical, including photocopying, recording, or by any information storage or retrieval systems, without permission in writing from the publisher. For information, contact:

Chelsea House
An imprint of Infobase Publishing
132 West 31st Street
New York NY 10001

Library of Congress Cataloging-in-Publication Data

Serradell, Joaquima.
  SARS / Joaquima Serradell ; consulting editor, Hilary Babcock ; foreword by David Heymann. — 2nd ed.
      p. cm. — (Deadly diseases and epidemics)
  Includes bibliographical references and index.
  ISBN-13: 978-1-60413-239-7 (hardcover : alk. paper)
  ISBN-10: 1-60413-239-6 (hardcover : alk. paper) 1. SARS (Disease) I. Babcock, Hilary. II. Title. III. Series.

  RC776.S27S47 2009
  616.2—dc22
                                   2009031056

Chelsea House books are available at special discounts when purchased in bulk quantities for businesses, associations, institutions, or sales promotions. Please call our Special Sales Department in New York at (212) 967-8800 or (800) 322-8755.

You can find Chelsea House on the World Wide Web at
http://www.chelseahouse.com

Text design by Terry Mallon
Illustrations by Dale Williams
Cover design by Takeshi Takahashi
Composition by Mary Susan Ryan-Flynn
Cover printed by Bang Printing, Brainerd, MN
Book printed and bound by Bang Printing, Brainerd, MN.
Date printed: December 2009
Printed in the United States of America

10 9 8 7 6 5 4 3 2 1

This book is printed on acid-free paper.

All links and Web addresses were checked and verified to be correct at the time of publication. Because of the dynamic nature of the Web, some addresses and links may have changed since publication and may no longer be valid.

Table of Contents

Foreword
David Heymann, World Health Organization   6

1. SARS: A Global Epidemic   8

2. SARS and Other Viral Infections   22

3. Spread and Symptoms of SARS   39

4. Diagnosis and Management of SARS   49

5. Treatment of SARS   62

6. Prevention and Public Health Measures   73

7. Impact and Significance of SARS   79

8. Lessons Learned from the SARS Epidemic   87

Appendix   98

Notes   101

Glossary   102

Bibliography   106

Further Resources   111

Index   112

About the Author   117

About the Consulting Editor   117

Communicable diseases kill and cause long-term disability. The microbial agents that cause them are dynamic, changeable, and resilient: They are responsible for more than 14 million deaths each year, mainly in developing countries.

Approximately 46 percent of all deaths in the developing world are due to communicable diseases, and almost 90 percent of these deaths are from AIDS, tuberculosis, malaria, and acute diarrheal and respiratory infections of children. In addition to causing great human suffering, these high-mortality communicable diseases have become major obstacles to economic development. They are a challenge to control either because of the lack of effective vaccines, or because the drugs that are used to treat them are becoming less effective because of antimicrobial drug resistance.

Millions of people, especially those who are poor and living in developing countries, are also at risk from disabling communicable diseases such as polio, leprosy, lymphatic filariasis, and onchocerciasis. In addition to human suffering and permanent disability, these communicable diseases create an economic burden—both on the workforce that handicapped persons are unable to join, and on their families and society, upon which they must often depend for economic support.

Finally, the entire world is at risk of the unexpected communicable diseases, those that are called emerging or re-emerging infections. Infection is often unpredictable because risk factors for transmission are not understood, or because it often results from organisms that cross the species barrier from animals to humans. The cause is often viral, such as Ebola and Marburg hemorrhagic fevers and severe acute respiratory syndrome (SARS). In addition to causing human suffering and death, these infections place health workers at great risk and are costly to economies. Infections such as Bovine Spongiform Encephalopathy (BSE) and the associated new human variant of Creutzfeldt-Jakob disease (vCJD) in Europe, and avian influenza A (H5N1) in Asia, are reminders of the seriousness of emerging and re-emerging infections. In addition, many of these infections have the potential to cause pandemics, which are a constant threat to our economies and public health security.

Science has given us vaccines and anti-infective drugs that have helped keep infectious diseases under control. Nothing demonstrates the effectiveness of vaccines better than the successful eradication of smallpox, the decrease in polio as the eradication program continues, and the decrease in measles when routine immunization programs are supplemented by mass vaccination campaigns.

Likewise, the effectiveness of anti-infective drugs is clearly demonstrated through prolonged life or better health in those infected with viral diseases such as AIDS, parasitic infections such as malaria, and bacterial infections such as tuberculosis and pneumococcal pneumonia.

But current research and development is not filling the pipeline for new anti-infective drugs as rapidly as resistance is developing, nor is vaccine development providing vaccines for some of the most common and lethal communicable diseases. At the same time, providing people with access to existing anti-infective drugs, vaccines, and goods such as condoms or bed nets—necessary for the control of communicable diseases in many developing countries—remains a great challenge.

Education, experimentation, and the discoveries that grow from them are the tools needed to combat high-mortality infectious diseases, diseases that cause disability, or emerging and re-emerging infectious diseases. At the same time, partnerships between developing and industrialized countries can overcome many of the challenges of access to goods and technologies. This book may inspire its readers to set out on the path of drug and vaccine development, or on the path to discovering better public health technologies by applying our current understanding of the human genome and those of various infectious agents. Readers may likewise be inspired to help ensure wider access to those protective goods and technologies. Such inspiration, with pragmatic action, will keep us on the winning side of the struggle against communicable diseases.

David L. Heymann
Assistant Director General
Health Security and Environment
Representative of the Director General for Polio Eradication
World Health Organization
Geneva, Switzerland

1

SARS:
A Global Epidemic

The significance of SARS as a public health threat is considerable. All new infectious diseases are poorly understood (by definition) as they emerge and are often associated with high mortality rates. SARS was no exception, and proved to be an especially difficult disease to diagnose and treat. Many new diseases have features that limit their potential for international spread. Some never establish efficient person-to-person transmission. Others depend on the presence of a mosquito or other vector as part of the transmission cycle. Still others remain closely tied to a specific geographical region or ecosystem. For some, patients are visibly too ill to travel during the most infectious period. In contrast, SARS passed readily from person to person, required no vector, had no particular geographic affinity, mimicked the symptoms of many other diseases, took its heaviest toll on hospital staff, killed around 11 percent of those infected, and spread internationally with alarming ease.[1]

THE PANIC BEGINS

In February 2003 a 48-year-old Chinese-American businessman named Johnny Cheng checked into the French Hospital in Hanoi, Vietnam. Three days before he got sick, he had arrived on a plane from Hong Kong, where he had stayed at the Metropole Hotel during his business trip. Now, he lay deathly ill in the hospital, where his condition baffled the doctors who examined him.

Cheng was showing symptoms of severe pneumonia. According to one nurse who treated him, "he was coughing a lot and developing a great amount of phlegm. In fact, he was coughing all night. . . ." But Cheng also showed other symptoms. He had severe shortness of breath and a high fever in addition to his cough, which led doctors to believe he was suffering from a more unusual disease.

Hoping for help in identifying the mysterious illness, the doctors called in infectious disease specialist Dr. Carlo Urbani, who worked for the World Health Organization (WHO). Urbani arrived at the French Hospital on February 28, and began a weeklong observation of Cheng's condition, during which he studied the man's symptoms and collected blood and saliva samples for analysis. Despite Urbani's work and the efforts of the hospital staff to save Cheng, relatives removed Cheng from the hospital and brought him back to Hong Kong, where he later died. Urbani, however, had succeeded in recognizing that he and his fellow medical experts were dealing with a new disease—not a common pneumonia. It got its own name—severe acute respiratory syndrome (or SARS) on March 15. By then, however, a great deal of damage had already been done.

On March 11, while flying to Bangkok, Thailand, to attend a conference, Dr. Urbani began to feel ill, and realized he was suffering from the same disease he had been observing in Johnny Cheng. Urbani moved quickly to isolate himself in a hospital to try to protect others from the disease. Over a period of several days, his condition grew worse, and his respiratory system collapsed. Ultimately, Urbani died of the very disease he had first identified and named.

Meanwhile, the new disease was continuing to spread—and to claim more lives. Five other medical workers at the French Hospital where Cheng had been treated died of SARS. Altogether, 62 cases in Vietnam were traced to Johnny Cheng. Cases also began to appear in people in Hong Kong, particularly those who had stayed at the Metropole Hotel during the time Cheng was there. By April 2003, many countries were reporting cases of similar pneumonia-like viral illnesses in patients, and people

DR. CARLO URBANI

Dr. Carlo Urbani, an epidemiologist and expert on **communicable diseases**, died of severe acute respiratory syndrome (SARS). Dr. Urbani worked in public health programs in Cambodia, Laos, and Vietnam, but was based in Hanoi, Vietnam.

Dr. Urbani was the first World Health Organization (WHO) officer to identify the outbreak of SARS, in the Chinese-American businessman who had been admitted to a small hospital in Hanoi. The patient had an unusual, influenza-like virus. Hospital officials in Hanoi asked whether someone from the WHO would examine the patient. Dr. Urbani answered that call. He suspected that the small hospital was facing something unusual. Dr. Urbani chose to work in the hospital, documenting findings, arranging for samples to be sent for testing, and reinforcing infection control. The hospital established an isolation ward that was kept under guard. Dr. Urbani worked directly with the medical staff of the hospital to strengthen morale and to keep fear in check as SARS revealed itself to be highly contagious and **virulent**. Of the first 60 patients who became infected with SARS, more than half were health care workers. To protect their families and community, some health care workers put themselves at great personal risk, deciding to sleep in the hospital, effectively sealing themselves off from the outside world.

Dr. Urbani did not survive to see the successes resulting from his early detection of SARS. On March 11, 2003, he began to have symptoms of the disease during a flight to Bangkok. On his arrival, he told his colleague from the Centers for Disease Control and Prevention (CDC) who greeted him at the airport not to approach him. They sat a distance from each other in silence, waiting for an ambulance to bring

were being quarantined all over the world to avoid spreading the disease. By December 2003, more than 800 people had died, and around 8,400 had been infected.

Figure 1.1 Dr. Carlo Urbani. (AP Images)

protective gear. Urbani fought SARS for the next 18 days in an isolation room in a Bangkok hospital. He died on March 29, 2003. Dr. Carlo Urbani was 46. He was married and the father of three children.

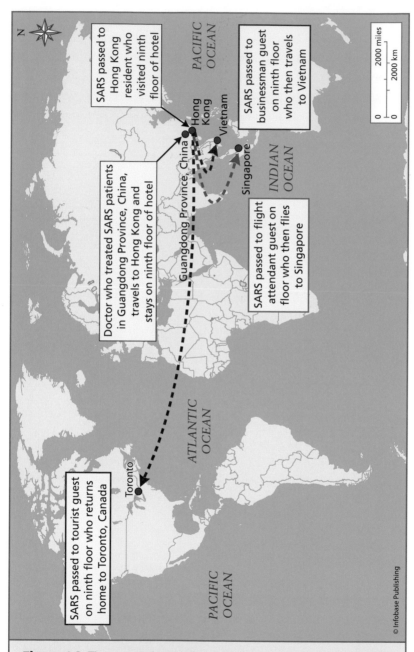

Figure 1.2 The ease and convenience of modern air travel enabled SARS to spread rapidly from its origin in a rural province of China to an industrialized area of Canada, halfway around the world. This map shows how particular people spread SARS in the early days of the outbreak in 2003.

As word got out about the potentially deadly new disease, the world was seized with panic. Headlines screamed warnings about the "Killer Bug," and people took personal precautions to fend off the dreaded illness. Throughout Asia and even in other parts of the world that had fewer cases of SARS, people began to wear surgical masks in public, hoping to avoid contaminated droplets from the air or the breath of other people. Some people refused to shake hands, afraid that the disease could be transmitted by touch. International travel slowed dramatically, especially to areas reporting cases of the disease. Toronto, Canada, which is usually a popular vacation spot for tourists from the United States, saw a 90 percent decline in its hotel and restaurant business after seven local people died and hundreds were quarantined in response to the SARS outbreak. Business conferences and even sporting events were canceled as people chose not to travel abroad if they could possibly avoid it.

Although the response of the media and general public may have been extreme, it is easy to understand the terrible fear that this deadly new viral disease caused. After the first reports of the illness in February 2003, SARS spread to more than two dozen countries in North America, South America, Europe, and Asia before the medical community was finally able to contain it. The vanishing of SARS was due to outstanding coordination efforts throughout the world and an aggressive response by the governments of the involved countries. Moreover, international agencies such as WHO worked heroically to rapidly identify and contain the disease.

WHAT IS SARS?

SARS is one of the new and very dangerous diseases of the twenty-first century, which include avian (bird) flu and Ebola. These diseases are caused by deadly viruses and may possibly be transmitted from animals to humans. SARS is caused by a special kind of **virus** called a **coronavirus** (CoV). It is very **infectious**—which means it is easily spread from one person to another. The virus remains active and is able to cause infection in both urine and feces for 24 to 48 hours. If a person with

SARS has diarrhea, his or her stool can harbor active viruses for up to four days! Even more frightening is the fact that the SARS virus can live for up to 24 hours without being inside a **host** (a person or animal whose cells it uses to function). It can contaminate surfaces—such as doorknobs or light switches—and if someone touches these surfaces within a few hours after an infected person touched them, he or she will risk contracting the virus. Scientists believe the virus's ability to contaminate

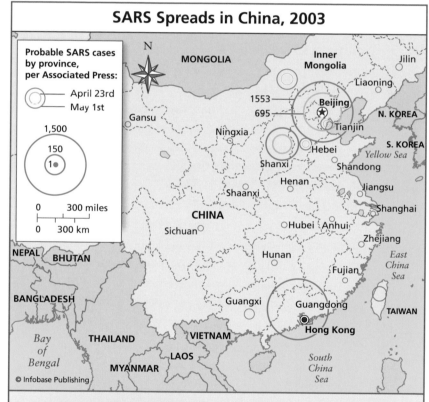

Figure 1.3 Although the first cases of SARS appeared in November 2002 and were limited to a small part of Guangdong Province, by April 2003 the new and mysterious disease had spread widely throughout China, and had even been found in the capital city of Beijing. This map shows the locations and numbers of SARS cases in various areas of China in the spring of 2003.

Figure 1.4 The outbreak of SARS in China and other parts of Asia caused many people around the world to abandon their travel plans to those areas, even before the World Health Organization issued its travel advisories suggesting that nonessential travel be avoided. Because of this dramatic decrease in travel to Asia, China and other nations took a tremendous economic hit. This photograph of a Chinese temple shows how places that were once filled with tourists were left virtually abandoned during the SARS epidemic. (AP Images)

inanimate objects for up to a full day explains in part why the virus was spread so quickly by people who flew in airplanes after the initial outbreak. Besides riding in an enclosed flight cabin with infected people, where air is continually recirculated, it might have been possible to get SARS by touching a contaminated meal tray or bathroom door.

THE ORIGINS AND SPREAD OF SARS

Scientists believe the SARS virus first cropped up in Guangdong Province, an agricultural area of southwestern China, where 80 million people live and work mainly as farmers. Many local residents practice traditional farming methods

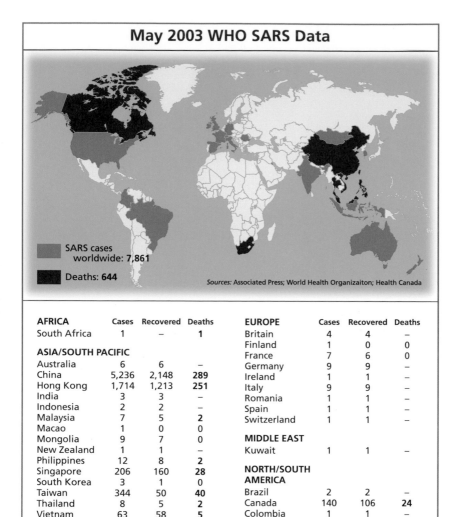

May 2003 WHO SARS Data

SARS cases worldwide: **7,861**

Deaths: **644**

Sources: Associated Press; World Health Organizaiton; Health Canada

AFRICA	Cases	Recovered	Deaths
South Africa	1	–	1
ASIA/SOUTH PACIFIC			
Australia	6	6	–
China	5,236	2,148	**289**
Hong Kong	1,714	1,213	**251**
India	3	3	–
Indonesia	2	2	–
Malaysia	7	5	**2**
Macao	1	0	0
Mongolia	9	7	0
New Zealand	1	1	–
Philippines	12	8	**2**
Singapore	206	160	**28**
South Korea	3	1	0
Taiwan	344	50	**40**
Thailand	8	5	**2**
Vietnam	63	58	**5**

EUROPE	Cases	Recovered	Deaths
Britain	4	4	–
Finland	1	0	0
France	7	6	0
Germany	9	9	–
Ireland	1	1	–
Italy	9	9	–
Romania	1	1	–
Spain	1	1	–
Switzerland	1	1	–
MIDDLE EAST			
Kuwait	1	1	–
NORTH/SOUTH AMERICA			
Brazil	2	2	–
Canada	140	106	**24**
Colombia	1	1	–
United States	67	34	0

© Infobase Publishing

Figure 1.5 The coordinated efforts of both national and international health agencies were successful in containing the SARS epidemic before it could spread far enough to infect or kill massive numbers of people. In May 2003, at the first meeting of the World Health Organization after the SARS outbreak began, WHO officials published the numbers of people who caught SARS and the numbers who died from it.

that keep them in close contact with animals such as chickens, ducks, fish, and pigs—all of which have been known to spread disease to humans. Although the rest of the world only learned about SARS between February and March 2003, towns in Guangdong had already recorded several cases of the mysterious new illness, starting as early as November 2002. The first SARS patient or the **index case** was believed to be a public servant living in the town of Foshan. Fortunately for him, he survived his battle with SARS, but he nonetheless managed to pass the disease on to at least four other people.

The earliest cases showed up as highly contagious and severe **atypical pneumonia**, and seemed to be affecting mainly health care workers and the members of their households. Many of the cases were rapidly fatal.

A doctor from Guangzhou, who had been treating some of the patients with the illness, may have been the one to spread SARS beyond Guangdong Province when he traveled to Hong Kong to attend a wedding. After he checked into the Metropole Hotel (the same place where businessman Johnny Cheng was staying), nine other guests were hospitalized with the symptoms of what later became known as SARS.

The Chinese government has long been known for trying to conceal bad news, even from its own people, so it was not surprising that officials worked hard to prevent word of the initial November outbreak from spreading in order to avoid causing a public panic and a possible economic crisis. Because of the delay in reporting the cases, however, people continued to travel normally and health workers did not always take the proper precautions to avoid becoming infected themselves. As a result, **clusters** of SARS cases began to pop up around the globe. By the end of March 2003, Hong Kong had seen a total of 320 cases over a period of under three weeks. Then, as infected people (particularly those who had been guests at the Metropole Hotel) resumed their travels, the disease was carried to Vietnam, Singapore, and Toronto, Canada.

In Vietnam, the outbreak was traced back to a man who was admitted to a hospital in Hanoi with high fever, dry cough, and mild sore throat. Following his admission, approximately 20 members of the hospital staff became sick with similar symptoms.

In Singapore, health authorities reported three cases of atypical pneumonia, one of which was a female flight attendant who had stayed at the Metropole Hotel. More than 100

THE WORLD HEALTH ORGANIZATION

The World Health Organization (WHO) is an international association established in 1948 with the goal of improving human health. WHO helps countries strengthen their health services, provides assistance in health emergencies, promotes disease prevention and control, and works to set international food safety, medical, and health standards.

According to the WHO's constitution, *health* is defined as a state of complete physical, mental, and social well-being—not merely the absence of disease or infirmity, which had been the way health was described for centuries before the WHO was founded.

The WHO is headquartered in Geneva, Switzerland, and governed by its 192 member states through the World Health Assembly. The main task of the World Health Assembly is to approve the WHO program and the budget and to decide policy questions.

In addition to its Geneva headquarters, the WHO has offices in most countries of the world, including six regional offices:

- Regional Office for Africa—located in Brazzaville, Republic of Congo

SARS cases in Singapore were ultimately traced back to this one woman.

Canadian health authorities informed international health agencies of a cluster of patients from a single hospital in Toronto. The disease came to Toronto with travelers who had flown in from Singapore.

Once the disease began to reach **epidemic** proportions, the Chinese were forced to admit, partly in response to pressure from the WHO, that there had been earlier cases in Guangdong. By March 2003, the WHO issued a global alert about cases of severe atypical pneumonia and mounting reports of cases among staff

- **Regional Office for Europe—located in Copenhagen, Denmark**

- **Regional Office for Southeast Asia—located in New Delhi, India**

- **Regional Office for the Americas/Pan American Health Organization—located in Washington, D.C.**

- **Regional Office for the Eastern Mediterranean—located in Cairo, Egypt**

- **Regional Office for the Western Pacific—located in Manila, Philippines.**

The WHO is probably best known for its successful campaign to eliminate the deadly disease smallpox, which had killed and maimed millions throughout history. By undertaking an intensive campaign to vaccinate people all over the world during the 1960s and 1970s, the WHO was able to eradicate smallpox as a naturally occurring disease. The last natural case of smallpox occurred in 1977. Today, smallpox exists only in scientific laboratories.

in certain Hanoi and Hong Kong hospitals. The health alert included a rare emergency travel advisory to international travelers, medical professionals, and health authorities, instructing all individuals traveling to affected areas to be watchful for the development of symptoms—including fever, headache, muscle stiffness, diarrhea, shortness of breath, and a dry cough—for a period of 10 days after their return.

According to the WHO, by August 2003, SARS had infected more than 8,422 people worldwide, and of these, 908 had died. In the United States, only eight people were confirmed to have been in contact with the SARS virus. All eight had traveled to other parts of the world where SARS had been spreading, but the people had not carried the illness to communities in the United States, a fact that is not yet fully understood. Heightened vigilance, control measures, and preparedness that followed the WHO's global alerts are thought to have contributed to the prevention of further significant outbreaks, and likely prevented what could have been a worldwide disaster that might have killed many thousands of people. The first global SARS epidemic was declared over by the WHO in August, 2003. No further human-to-human transmission has taken place. Isolated outbreaks have occurred since then due to accidental releases of the SARS-CoV isolates from laboratories in Taiwan, Singapore, and China. A recurrence of a SARS epidemic may occur in the future. Understanding the pathogenesis and the molecular transmission of SARS are paramount in finding effective treatments.

THE DEATH TOLL

Mortality (the number of people in a given population who die from an illness, in this case, SARS) was initially believed to be around 3 percent, but may, in fact, be as high as 15 percent. The WHO estimates that the **case fatality rate** (the proportion of people with a disease who die from the disease within a given period of time) for SARS ranges from 0 percent to 50 percent. The older the age group, the higher the fatality rate. In general, children experience a mild form of the disease with an extremely low death rate. Mortality rates are highest among the elderly and people who have weakened immune systems or are already struggling with other diseases. Elderly people are more likely to die from a SARS infection because they have reduced lung function that comes with age, as well as less efficient immune systems.

HOW SARS WAS CONTAINED

Measures to contain SARS (prevent it from spreading) took two major forms: **isolation** of symptomatic cases (people who showed obvious symptoms of the disease) to prevent transmission, and **quarantine** (the close observation of **asymptomatic** contacts—people who did not show symptoms but might have been infected—so that they could be isolated immediately if they did begin to show signs of the disease). Along with travel restrictions and advisories, the close watch kept on SARS patients was responsible to a large extent for stopping the further spread of the disease.

The terrifyingly rapid spread of a new and previously unidentified—and incurable—virus made the global medical community realize that, despite great advances in preventing and treating illness over the last century, the threat of infectious disease has not gone away. SARS has made all of us aware that deadly **pathogens** (disease-causing organisms) still exist and that it takes the cooperation of the entire world to stop them from killing huge numbers of people.

2

SARS and Other Viral Infections

Wow, that was a close call! I didn't realize that my dad was in such danger, but now that I understand a little more about viruses and infections, it all makes perfect sense.

My name is Paul. I'm a junior in high school. It's not that I don't love my folks, but they aren't very exciting. My dad sells paper clips—not a particularly glamorous career. Dad certainly never had his picture in the newspaper—at least not until last week.

Something happened last week that changed our lives. Dad was on a flight to Singapore, where he buys many of the paper clip products he sells. He noticed that several of the other passengers had really bad coughs. Ordinarily, he wouldn't even have given that fact a second thought, but earlier, during the same flight, he had read an article about SARS (severe acute respiratory syndrome), and all the coughing had made him a little worried.

He mentioned his concerns to the flight attendant, who said that it was nothing to worry about—people cough on every flight. She suggested that my dad just relax. But Dad wasn't satisfied with that response. He walked around and wrote down the seat numbers of the people who were coughing, along with a brief physical description of each person. After the plane landed, Dad gave his information to the health officers at the immigration office. They treated him politely, but they probably thought he was a little crazy for being so concerned about a few people coughing.

It turned out that Dad had been right for worrying. The very next day, one of the coughers from the airplane went to the emergency room at the hospital in Singapore with a high fever, chills, and difficulty breathing. He was diagnosed as having SARS and was immediately isolated in the **quarantine** *ward, so he would not infect anyone else. The authorities asked him to name all the people with whom he had been in close contact over the last few days, but that was impossible. He didn't know the names of any of the 204 other passengers from the flight he'd been on the day before. Luckily, a health officer at the airport immigration office remembered the man—my dad—who had come in with the list of coughing passengers. They found the list, rounded up the eight passengers, and isolated them all until they were no longer contagious.*

Dad had stopped a serious SARS **outbreak** *from happening. It could have affected up to 100,000 people in the country and caused as many as 15,000 deaths. The prime minister of Singapore gave my dad a medal of honor in a public ceremony of thanks. Dad was also featured on the cover of* TIME *magazine and on the front page of our local newspaper,* The Guardian.

Now, the phone doesn't stop ringing. Reporters want to interview Dad, and they even try to speak with me to get my thoughts about having such a thoughtful and clever father.

After my dad's amazing experience, I listen to him when he gives advice about paying attention to what's going on around me! Being observant helped my dad prevent a dangerous disease from spreading and may have saved a lot of lives.*

Infection is defined as a disease resulting from the presence of certain **microorganisms** (living things that are too small to be seen without a microscope) in the body. These organisms (commonly called "germs") can be single-celled amoebas, bacteria, or tiny viruses. Usually, they enter our bodies through our mouth and nose when we breathe, eat contaminated foods, or come into close contact with an infected

*Fictional narrative

(continues on page 26)

LOUIS PASTEUR

Louis Pasteur was born in 1822 in Dole, France. He was trained as a research chemist and became so well known and respected that, in 1854, at age 32, he became dean of the Faculty of Science at the University of Lille. At this time, Lille was the center of alcohol manufacturing in France.

A local industrialist asked Pasteur to look at his beer factory, where many of his vats of fermented beer were turning sour. After using a microscope to analyze samples from the vats, Pasteur found thousands of microorganisms. He was convinced that they were responsible for the beer going sour. Pasteur believed that they were the cause, rather than the result, of the putrid beer. Pasteur went on to study wine and milk as well as beer.

Figure 2.1 Louis Pasteur. (Omikron/Photo Researchers, Inc.)

In 1865, he was asked to investigate his first disease, called *pebrine*, which affected the silkworm industry. Pasteur discovered that the disease was caused by a living organism, and he became convinced that microbes could affect humans as well as beer, milk, and worms.

In this sense, Pasteur believed that microbes could spread diseases among humans. He developed his work by finding out ways humans could avoid getting diseases. He knew about the work done by Edward Jenner in inoculating people against smallpox. Pasteur reasoned that if a vaccine could be found for smallpox, then a vaccine could likely be found for all diseases.

In 1880, he found a vaccine by chance. His assistant, Chamberland, had inoculated some chickens with chicken cholera germs from an old culture that had been around for some time. The chickens did not die. Pasteur asked Chamberland to repeat what he had done but with a fresh culture of chicken cholera germs. Pasteur reasoned that a new culture would provide more potent germs. Two groups of chickens were inoculated; one group had previously been given the old culture and another had not. Those chickens that had been inoculated with the old culture survived the new inocculation, and those that had not died. The chickens that had been inoculated with the old culture had become immune to chicken cholera.

In addition, Pasteur and his team studied the disease rabies. Most human victims of rabies died a painful death. Although the team could not identify the germ that caused rabies, they did learn that the rabies germ attacked the nervous system only after it had made its way to the brain. The team then traced the germ to the brain and spinal cord of infected animals and, by using dried spinal cords, they produced a vaccine for rabies.

Louis Pasteur's name is forever cemented in the history of medicine because he showed that microbes were the cause of disease and because his work helped lead to the development of many useful vaccines.

(continued from page 23)

person. They can also enter through the eyes or be transmitted sexually. Microorganisms can also get inside our bodies through cuts or open wounds.

GERM THEORY AND DISEASE

In the late nineteenth century, scientists came up with the **germ theory** of disease. It states that many diseases are caused by microorganisms and that microorganisms grow through reproduction rather than being spontaneously generated. This new understanding helped scientists see how infectious microorganisms could cause disease in humans. Now, they just had to find and isolate the specific organisms that caused particular diseases to have a better idea of how the illness might be treated or prevented.

In identifying agents that cause human disease, Robert Koch (1843–1910), a German country doctor, came up with a method by which an organism could be isolated from (taken out of) a sick animal or person, grown in the laboratory, and then used to infect a healthy individual who would develop the same disease and carry the same organism. Using this method, Koch helped scientists understand the nature of infectious diseases, and the ways in which they were transmitted between people and between animals and people. Koch's most influential contributions to medicine were the isolation of the tubercule bacillus (the cause of tuberculosis) and the establishment of the essential steps (known as "Koch's postulates" required to prove that an organism is the cause of disease.

WHAT IS A VIRUS?

A virus is a very small infectious organism—much smaller than a bacterium, another common disease-causing microorganism. Also unlike bacteria, viruses need a living cell in order to reproduce. In fact, some scientists do not even consider viruses to be living things. Because they are so small, they have very few components, and must be precisely packaged.

A typical virus consists of genetic material surrounded by a protein coat, or **capsid**. Viruses contain nucleic acid, which can be made up of **RNA (ribonucleic acid)** or **DNA (deoxyribonucleic acid)** or both, and may be single- or double-stranded, and either circular or linear.

The virus's goal is to find a place where it can set up a "home" for itself and make many copies of its own genetic material. This is the virus's sole reason for existence. To achieve this goal, the virus invades the body of a living creature and attaches to one of its cells, which is then called the host cell. Once inside a cell, the virus releases its DNA or RNA, which contains the information needed to create new virus particles. By doing this, the virus essentially takes over the cell's usual function and forces it to make more virus particles instead of doing its regular job. At this point, the cell is said to be infected by the virus.

What ultimately happens to the invaded cell depends on the type of virus that attacks it. Some viruses kill the cells they infect. Others just alter the cell's function so that the cell loses control over its normal process of cell division. Some viruses incorporate a part or all of their genetic information into the host cell's DNA. Once inside the cell, the virus uses the cell's machinery to **replicate** (multiply) while putting regular cellular processes on hold.

VIRUSES AND HOSTS

Viruses usually have a certain kind of host they prefer to live in. Some, such as the influenza virus, can infect humans and a variety of other animals. Most viruses that are commonly found in people, however, are spread from person to person directly, not from animals to people. Other viruses, such as the rabies virus or encephalitis viruses, infect animals primarily and humans only occasionally. Viruses are referred to as intracellular parasites. That is, they need to be inside a specific type of live host cell to allow them to produce energy and replicate. Without a proper host, they cannot survive for long, if at all.

The SARS Coronavirus

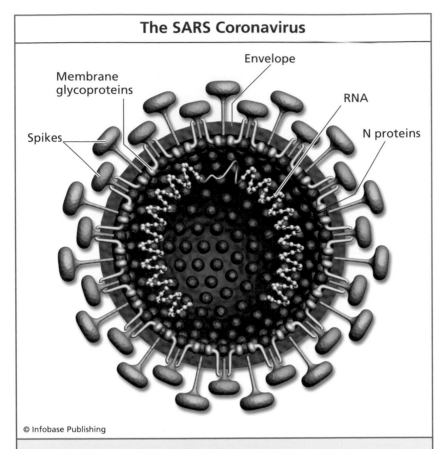

Membrane glycoproteins

Envelope

RNA

N proteins

Spikes

© Infobase Publishing

Figure 2.2 Viruses are tiny particles made up of little more than genetic material and a protein coat (like the virus illustrated here). Although they contain nucleic acids—either RNA or DNA—which all living cells need to reproduce, many scientists argue that viruses are not living things at all, because a virus cannot reproduce on its own. To multiply it essentially has to "hijack" a host cell and use the cell's machinery to make new virus particles.

HOW VIRUSES CAUSE INFECTION

There are three requirements that must be met if a virus is going to successfully cause an infection. First, there must be enough of the virus present to cause infection. Different viruses need to be present in different amounts to infect a host. Second, the host cells must be susceptible to the virus. This means that the host must not be immune to the virus, like someone who has received a vaccination to prevent a certain disease would be. Finally, the host's local defenses must be absent when the virus attacks.

The body has a number of specific and nonspecific defenses against viruses and other pathogens. Physical barriers such as the skin and mucous membranes discourage easy entry into the body. Infected cells also make **interferon**, a special type of protein that can make noninfected cells more resistant to infection by many viruses. However, if a virus does enter the body, various types of white blood cells, such as lymphocytes, are able to attack and destroy infected cells. The outcome of virus infection varies depending on the virus. In some cases, there is little impact on the cell, and in other cases, the cell dies.

THE HUMAN IMMUNE SYSTEM

The human body is designed to help protect us against disease. It has several different ways to do this.

The body's first line of defense consists of physical barriers that act to keep pathogens (like viruses) from getting inside the cells. Among these barriers are the skin, the mucous membranes (which can trap pathogens in sticky mucus and expel them from the body), and **cilia** (hairlike structures in the nose, lungs, and other organs that help sweep foreign substances out of the body). Before it can mount a successful infection, the SARS virus must get past these physical defenses. Because it is carried in the breath of infected people, a person can breathe in the virus in the air, and it is carried to the lungs, where it can start an infection. It may also be able to get into the body through cuts or open wounds on the skin.

Once a foreign organism gets inside the body, the immune system launches another set of defense mechanisms. The immune system is made up of many different kinds of cells that play very special roles in destroying invaders and helping the body repair itself from damage done by infectious organisms. Among the immune cells that attack first are **macrophages**—large cells that literally gobble up invading organisms and kill them. (*Macro* refers to the large part of a cell, while *phage* means "eater of.")

But macrophages cannot eliminate an invader entirely on their own. So, the immune system also has white blood cells, or lymphocytes, that help stop an infection.

B cells, one type of lymphocyte, travel through the bloodstream, looking for foreign organisms. When they encounter cells they do not recognize, they attach to them and produce **antibodies**—proteins that will remain in the body and help it to recognize a particular pathogen quickly in the event of a future attack.

Meanwhile, T cells, another type of lymphocyte, also take part in the immune defense. There are two types of T cells. Regular, or helper, T cells locate invading pathogens and send out chemical signals to the rest of the body to let the immune system know an invasion is taking place. Killer T cells, on the other hand, not only recognize invaders, but also have the ability to attach to and destroy unfamiliar cells—whether these cells are viruses, bacteria, or even cancerous cells of the body's own tissues.

Together, these immune system cells are very good at keeping the body healthy, but they can be outnumbered when enough viruses or other pathogens enter and begin to infect the cells. And some pathogens have developed special tricks to evade the immune system. Once an infection begins, it can take the immune system a long time, from days to weeks or even months, to completely destroy the invaders and end the infection. The faster an infection takes hold, the more dangerous it can be. And the SARS virus often infects with lightning speed.

TYPES OF VIRUSES

There are four main types of viruses:

- **Icosahedral:** This kind of virus has an outer shell (capsid) made from 20 flat sides, which gives the virus a spherical shape. Most viruses are icosahedral.

- **Helical:** This type of virus has a capsid that is shaped like a rod.

- **Enveloped:** In these viruses, the capsid is encased in a baggy membrane, which can change shape but often looks spherical.

- **Complex:** A complex virus has its genetic material coated, but does not have a capsid.

Among the enveloped type of viruses is the **coronavirus**, which is responsible for SARS. The first known coronavirus was isolated from chickens in 1937.

SARS: A CORONAVIRUS

Severe acute respiratory syndrome (SARS) is caused by a previously unknown coronavirus, now called SARS-associated coronavirus (SARS-CoV).

Coronaviruses get their name because of the way they look. They appear to have a halo or crown (*corona* in Latin) when viewed under a microscope. Coronavirus particles are irregularly shaped with an outer envelope that has distinctive, "club-shaped" **peplomers** (a subunit of a virus particle). Coronaviruses are RNA (ribonucleic acid) viruses that replicate in the cytoplasm of the animal host cells, and cause disease in humans and animals, including the common cold. Coronavirus infections are very common and occur worldwide. The **incidence** of infection is strongly seasonal, with its greatest incidence among children in winter. Adult infections are less frequent. Coronaviruses can occasionally cause more severe disease, such as pneumonia, but this is rare. In fact, before SARS was discovered, the human coronaviruses previously known were only associated with mild diseases. SARS-related CoV seems to be the first coronavirus that regularly causes potentially fatal illness in humans.

The SARS virus is very hardy and can survive in the environment without being inside a host for several hours. All viruses have short lives when not attached to a living cell.

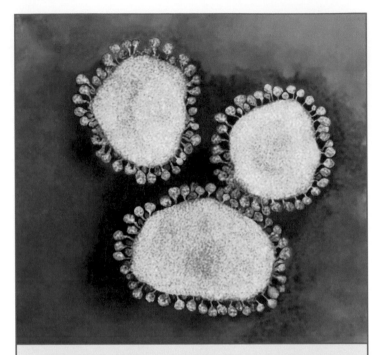

Figure 2.3 SARS coronaviruses, as seen through an electron microscope. With the extraordinary detail the magnification produces, it is easy to see the "halo" that surrounds the virus, and the stubby peplomers that protrude from its surface. (Dr. Linda Stannard, UCT/Photo Researchers, Inc.)

The new SARS coronavirus has some unusual properties. For one, the SARS virus can be grown in Vero cells (a cell line isolated in 1962 from a primate). This is an unusual characteristic of **HCoVs (human coronaviruses)**, most of which cannot be cultivated. You might wonder, if coronaviruses usually cause only mild illness in humans, then how can this new coronavirus be responsible for a potentially life-threatening disease like SARS? Because the SARS virus is so recently identified, there is not yet enough information about it to determine the full range of illnesses that it might be able to cause. Coronaviruses have occasionally been linked to pneumonia in humans, especially in people with weakened immune systems. The viruses can also cause severe disease in animals. Could the SARS virus have evolved from an animal virus?

Figure 2.4 The masked palm civet (whose technical name is *Paguma larvata*) is a small animal related to the mongoose. Its natural habitat ranges from Asia's Himalayan Mountains to Indonesia. In many parts of Asia, and particularly in China, the masked palm civet is considered a gourmet delicacy. Because this creature has been shown to have antibodies to SARS-like viruses, scientists at first believed the disease may have been spread to humans when people ate contaminated civets. (Reuters/Corbis)

THE SEARCH FOR THE CAUSE OF SARS

Dr. Malik Peiris and his colleagues at the University of Hong Kong were the first to identify a new type of coronavirus from two patients with SARS. They then found evidence of the same virus in 90 percent of the 50 patients they studied. The new coronavirus, which is responsible for SARS, is called SARS-CoV, short for SARS–human coronavirus.

A number of laboratories across the world undertook the job of determining what kind of virus was causing SARS. The virus isolation was performed on a specimen from a person from the original case cluster from Toronto, Canada, who had died of the disease. A bronchoalveolar lavage was performed. This is a process in which a long flexible tube is inserted through a patient's mouth and down their throat into their airway. Water is squirted into the respiratory tract and then the fluid is suctioned out and cultured in a growth medium to search for any pathogens that may be living in the respiratory tract. The National Microbiology Laboratory in Canada isolated the virus from a patient in Toronto and succeeded in growing a coronavirus-like agent in African green monkey cells.

This coronavirus was named publicly by the World Health Organization and cooperating laboratories on April 16, 2003, as the "SARS virus." The efforts of laboratories from 10 countries, together with WHO, helped speed up the identification of the SARS virus after the test of causation, including monkey inoculation. To prove causation—that is, to declare definitively that the new coronavirus was the cause of SARS—the virus had to go through all four of Koch's postulates for proving the causation of disease. As you will recall, the pathogen must be found in all cases of the disease, must be isolated from the host and grown in pure culture, must reproduce the original disease when introduced into a susceptible host, and must be found in the experimental host that was infected. In SARS patients the novel coronavirus has been found in patients' bodily fluids. The virus has been cultured in an artificial culture. The cultured virus produces disease in monkeys (macaque monkeys). And lastly, the virus can be isolated from the infected monkey. This is the process by which scientists have proven that SARS is caused by the new coronavirus SARS-CoV.

STUDYING THE VIRUS

Research in China and Hong Kong detected several corona-viruses that are closely related genetically to SARS-CoV in two animal species (masked palm civet and raccoon dog) and anti-bodies against SARS-CoV in one additional species (Chinese ferret badger). These and other wild animals are traditionally considered delicacies and are sold as food for human consumption in markets throughout southern China. It became obvious to scientists that eating these infected animals was likely what spread the disease to humans. Isolating viruses from these animals indicated that the SARS virus can exist outside of a human host.

The **genome** sequence data of SARS reveal that the new agent does not belong to any of the previously known groups of coronaviruses, including the two known human coronaviruses. It seems that the new SARS virus supports the hypothesis that it is an animal virus for which the normal host is still unknown and that has recently either developed the ability to infect humans or has been able to cross the species barrier.

SARS' ANIMAL ORIGINS

The SARS outbreak in China in Guangdong Province is believed to have started when humans became infected as they raised and slaughtered wild animals for food or bought and sold them at a market. Coronaviruses that are 99 percent similar genetically to the surface spike protein of human SARS isolates have been found in Guangdong from apparently healthy masked palm civets, a catlike mammal closely related to the mongoose. It is possible that people first got SARS by eating these local animals.

Sampling of several animals species in one of the animal markets in Guandong showed that some of them carried a virus genetically related to the human SARS coronavirus. It was suspected that the animal precursor of SARS was originally not very efficient at infecting humans. The history of exposure from the first victims of the disease revealed that the live-animal markets were probably the site where the transfer of the animal virus to humans occurred. The reservoir of the virus was thought to be the palm civet or the raccoon dog sold in Chinese markets. However, those two animals may have just been the carrier of the disease in the live-animal markets, without becoming ill themselves. There could be other reservoirs of the virus in other species in the wild.[1, 2]

Recently, bats have been suspected of being the natural reservoir for SARS. Bats rarely display clinical symptoms of diseases even though they often have persistent infections with multiple viruses. The increased use of bats or products from bats in food and traditional medicine in southern China and other parts of Asia reinforces this theory.

SARS-CoV MOLECULAR FINDINGS

More recent research into the molecular and biological processes of the SARS virus helps to explain the disease. SARS is caused by a coronavirus. Its genome is a positive single-stranded ribonucleic acid (RNA) containing 14 functional **open reading frames (ORFs)**. Two of the large ORFs constitute the **replicase** gene, which encodes proteins required for viral RNA syntheses. The remaining 12 ORFs encode the four structural proteins found in the SARS coronavirus: spike, membrane, **nucleocapsid**, and envelope. The RNA is surrounded by nucleocapsid (N). The N protein plays an essential role in the SARS-CoV genome packaging and **virion** (viral particle) assembly. It is

Figure 2.5 The Chinese horseshoe bat has been identified as a carrier of the SARS virus. (Courtesy Gareth Jones, School of Biological Sciences, University of Bristol, UK)

itself surrounded by membrane (M) proteins. The envelope contains spike (S) proteins.

It is now known that the S protein plays a pivotal role in the transmission of SARS. The cellular entry of enveloped viruses (such as SARS-CoV) often depends on attachment proteins found on the host cell surfaces. Viral envelope proteins bind with these receptors in ways that are not completely known, facilitating fusion of the host cell's and the viral membranes to introduce viral contents into the cell. SARS virions attach to host cell surface receptors via their spike (S) proteins. Once its contents are in the host cell, the virus genome can replicate. The human host cell receptor for SARS-CoV has been identified as the **angiotensin converting enzyme 2**

(ACE2) receptor. The S protein attaches the virus to its cellular receptor, ACE2, triggering the membrane fusion between virus and its host cells.

The specificity of receptor binding is of vital importance in explaining the process of infecting host cells. Further, it allows the possibility of designing specific drugs against SARS that might block viral-to-host cell membrane fusion and therefore neutralize the virus.

3

Spread and Symptoms of SARS

SARS is a communicable disease and a very contagious one that can have fatal consequences. Communicable diseases are illnesses that are transmitted between people either directly, or indirectly through an intermediate animal, host, or vector. (A vector is anything that transmits a disease to another living thing.) The main means by which SARS appears to spread is close person-to-person contact, primarily through the respiratory droplets an infected person produces when he or she coughs or sneezes. The disease can spread when droplets from the cough or sneeze of an infected person are propelled a short distance (generally up to 3 feet [1 meter]) through the air and enter the mouth, nose, or eyes of anyone who happens to be nearby. For infection to occur, however, scientists believe the droplets in the air would have to contain extremely large numbers of the SARS virus. The virus can also spread when a person touches a surface or object that has been contaminated with such infectious droplets and then touches his or her mouth, nose, or eyes.

The airborne spread of SARS—such as from a cough—does not seem to be the major route of transmission, except in situations where people are exposed frequently to massive amounts of pathogens in the air, as occurred in the hospitals where the first SARS patients were treated. **Airborne** (moving by or though the air) **transmission** of the SARS virus is probably a relatively rare event. SARS cases among health care workers show that most of those infected were exposed to the virus during high-risk activities such as **endotracheal intubation, bronchoscopy,** and **sputum induction,** all of which involves accessing a patient's airway and

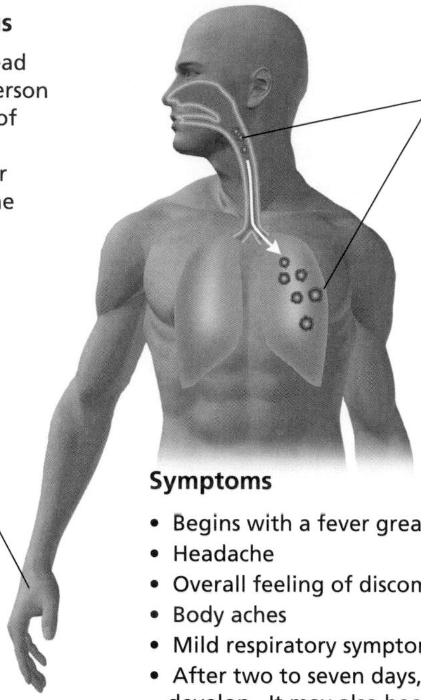

Symptoms and Spread of SARS

Spreading the virus

SARS appears to spread by close person-to-person contact. Most cases of SARS have involved people who cared for or lived with someone with the virus.

The virus can also spread by touching contaminated surfaces then touching your eyes, nose, or mouth.

SARS can spread through respiratory droplets released by coughing and sneezing. SARS may also spread through the air or in ways that are currently unknown.

Inside the body

The virus replicates in the respiratory tract and moves down into the lungs, possibly leading to severe respiratory distress.

Symptoms

- Begins with a fever greater than 100.4° F
- Headache
- Overall feeling of discomfort
- Body aches
- Mild respiratory symptoms
- After two to seven days, a dry cough may develop. It may also become more difficult to breathe.

Sources: Centers for Disease Control and Prevention; World Health Organization.
© Infobase Publishing

Figure 3.1 SARS is a highly contagious disease that typically begins with a high fever.

may cause excessive coughing. This means that it is suspected that they contracted the disease from the instruments used on SARS patients, not directly through the air from patients themselves.

HOW THE SARS VIRUS WORKS

The study of changes in organs, such as lungs and intestines, of SARS patients contributed to a better understanding of the **pathogenesis** of SARS, or the way the virus causes disease. Autopsies of SARS patients have revealed that the predominant finding was diffuse damage in the lung tissue. This severe pulmonary injury is caused both by direct and indirect viral effects and by the immune response to the virus. Additional changes include **squamous metaplasia** of bronchial and alveolar **epithelial** cells; **subpleural prolifera-tion** of **fibrogranulative tissue** in small airways, and the loss of **cilia** of bronchiolar epithelial cells. In a number of SARS cases, co-infections have been detected with bacteria such as *Pseudomonas aeruginosa* and fungi such as *Aspergillus*. Moreover, in most SARS autopsies extensive **necrosis**, or tissue death, in the spleen, kidneys, and other organs is also commonly found.

Studies of the tissue and cellular distribution of SARS-CoV, and ACE2 protein expression, show that ACE2 is expressed at high levels in the primary target cells of SARS-CoV, that is in cells lining airways in the lung and those lining the small intes-tine. It is also suspected that other co-receptors may play a role in the interaction between the virus and its target cells in other organs of the SARS patient.

The role of the innate immune response in the pathogen-esis of SARS has been recently determined. The **innate immune system** is the first line of defense against viruses. During most viral infections, most cell types in the body respond by secreting high levels of type 1 **interferon** as a line of defense. This does not happen in the case of a SARS-CoV infection. The immune-related genes that are overexpressed after the onset of SARS are usually associated with the innate immune response against a bacterial infection and not against a viral one. The response of SARS patients is mainly an innate **inflammatory** response rather than the specific immune response that is normally seen in a viral infection. It has been suggested that the SARS virus may cause deficiencies in the innate response. A compromised immune response may lead to proliferation of SARS-CoV with more severe injuries and more widespread organ damage.

EXPOSURE TO SARS

In the context of SARS, close contact means having cared for or lived with someone infected with SARS or having direct contact with the respiratory secretions and/or body fluids of a patient known to have SARS. Examples include kissing or embracing, sharing eating or drinking utensils, talking to someone within a space of about 3 feet, physical examination, and any other direct physical contact between people. Close contact does not include activities such as walking past a person or briefly sitting across from someone in a waiting room or office.

The presence of the SARS virus in the stool suggests that **oral-fecal transmission** is also one possibility. An outbreak in an apartment complex in Hong Kong that accounted for more than 300 cases was attributed to fecal spread. The SARS-CoV is stable in feces (and urine) at room temperature for at least one to two days.

Part of what determines whether someone who is exposed to SARS will get sick is the size of the **inoculum**—that is, the number of infectious particles that are transmitted from the infected person to the healthy person. The size of the inoculum is determined by the **viral load** (number of viruses) in the secretions of the infected patient and the distance the healthy person is from the index patient. When someone first contracts SARS, the viral load is relatively low for the first few days after the onset of symptoms. The viral load increases gradually, peaking on the tenth day after the first symptoms appear. This suggests that SARS patients may be most contagious around the tenth day of the disease. They may be more or less likely to spread the illness the rest of the time, even during the symptomatic phase of the disease.

SYMPTOMS

The first symptoms of SARS are nonspecific—which means that they are very similar to the symptoms of many other diseases. This makes it hard for doctors to make a diagnosis. Symptoms start out with flulike complaints, including high fever (above 100.4°F, or 38.0°C). This fever is often accompanied by headaches, malaise (a general feeling of being unwell), chills, and diarrhea.

Because these common symptoms make it difficult to distinguish SARS from an ordinary infection of the airways, such as bronchitis, doctors have to do a clinical examination of the patient along with radiological (X-ray) and laboratory tests to tell if the person really does have SARS. Anyone who comes down with flulike symptoms and has had prior contact with someone known to have SARS, or has traveled to a geographic location where SARS is relatively common, should seek medical attention immediately upon noticing symptoms.

When a person is infected with SARS, it may take between two and ten days for symptoms to appear. This is typically the virus's **incubation period**—the time between the entry of the

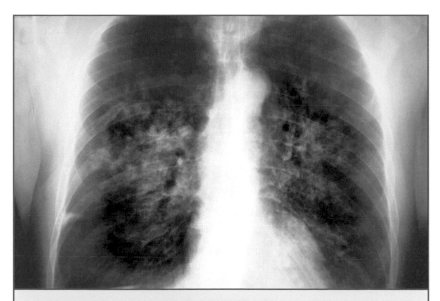

Figure 3.2 X-ray of patient with SARS infection. SARS causes severe inflammation of the lungs, which can lead to respiratory distress, pulmonary fibrosis (scarring of the lungs), and lung failure. (Philippe Garo/Photo Researchers, Inc.)

disease organism into the body and when symptoms first show up. After the initial symptoms, either the disease subsides, or it progresses to a severe respiratory phase. This second phase is dangerous and can lead to acute respiratory failure and death. The respiratory phase starts within two to four days of the onset of fever. A dry, nonproductive cough develops and may be accompanied by shortness of breath. This usually takes place during the second week of the illness. Sometimes SARS progresses to a generalized infection of the lung, and the patient requires intubation (the passing of a tube into the lung so that oxygen may be provided to ease breathing difficulty) and mechanical ventilation just to survive. In such cases, a machine sends oxygen under pressure into the lungs and removes the carbon dioxide from the respiratory system. In severe cases, like that of Dr. Carlo Urbani, even these measures may not be enough to save the person's life.

WHO CAN SPREAD SARS?

For easy and efficient transmission of the SARS virus, the "ideal" conditions would be to have a patient who is highly infectious, shedding (passing out of the body through the breath, urine, or feces) large quantities of infectious virus. The patient must also have comorbidities (other illnesses) that mask the symptoms and signs of SARS. Patients with other chronic conditions and weakened immune systems will be most vulnerable. Finally, the patient has to be somewhere where he or she can expose a lot of other people. This can happen when a SARS patient is admitted to a hospital and put into contact with multiple persons through the diagnostic testing process, possibly including high-risk procedures such as bronchoscopy, intubation, and use of **nebulizers**.

It is still unclear whether someone who is infected but asymptomatic can infect others. There is no direct evidence that transmission of SARS has ever occurred from an asymptomatic person. Indirect evidence that this may occur in rare cases includes a report that tracing contacts of SARS patients in Hong Kong failed to identify a known symptomatic SARS patient in a small percentage of reported cases. But this could also be a result of an incomplete search for contacts.

Scientists generally believe that only patients who currently show symptoms spread the SARS virus efficiently. However, transmission appears not to happen in an explosive way. Some 81 percent of all probable SARS patients in Singapore showed no evidence that they had spread SARS or any other clinically identifiable illness to other people.

This information fits with observations from the early Toronto outbreak, when suspected cases in which people did not seem to have pneumonia were initially sent home to spend their time in isolation. Some patients did not adhere to the isolation requirements and went out and interacted with the community. Despite this fact, apart from an outbreak among a religious group, no additional disease turned up in the community. Also, a report from the Philippines describes a patient who began to show symptoms on April 6, had close contact with 254 family members and friends, traveled extensively through the Philippines, and attended a prayer meeting and a wedding before being hospitalized on April 12. The people with whom the patient had been in contact were placed under home quarantine for nine days, with twice-daily temperature monitoring by health workers to help authorities determine if any new cases turned up that could be traced back to the first patient. Elevated temperature is the first warning sign. Of all the exposed contacts, only two individuals developed SARS. This figure represents an infection rate of less than 1 percent for contacts made outside of the hospital setting. Compared with other infectious diseases that may be spread via the respiratory route—for example, influenza—SARS may sometimes be only moderately transmissible through the air.

SUPERSPREADING

The term *superspreading* has been used to describe situations in which a single individual has directly infected a large number of other people. In the Singapore epidemic, of the first 201 probable SARS cases reported, 103 of the patients had been infected by just five source patients.

A common feature of superspreading is **nosocomial** (happening in the hospital) transmission, with hospitals serving as sources for the spread and increase in severity of the disease. The most probable explanation for the phenomenon of superspreading is extensive viral shedding by particular patients. Any infected patient releases virus into the environment around them as he or she breathes. This is referred to as "viral shedding." Some people may release much higher quantities of the virus than others, though, perhaps because they are in an advanced stage of the disease or have other illnesses that allow the virus to multiply even faster than usual.

RECOGNIZING AN ILLNESS AS SARS

Unrecognized cases of SARS have been implicated in outbreaks in Singapore, Taiwan, and Toronto. Despite efforts to implement extensive control measures, these outbreaks happened, and spread to other health care facilities. Several factors might contribute to the difficulties in recognizing cases of SARS. For one, early SARS symptoms are nonspecific and patients may seem to be suffering from other, more common illnesses. Moreover, patients may have chronic conditions, and their SARS symptoms might be attributed to those underlying diseases. Finally, some patients might not reveal useful information for fear of being stigmatized—that is, feeling ashamed of having the disease. These experiences demonstrate that the spread of SARS among health care workers can occur despite medical professionals' knowledge about how SARS is transmitted.

There has been at least one report of SARS-CoV transmission during **quarantine**. Family contacts of a SARS patient became infected during hospital quarantine because strict isolation was not enforced. Patients diagnosed with SARS may or may not be infected with the SARS virus, but they are certainly at risk of contracting the infection if they are grouped with known infected SARS patients. Therefore, individual isola-

HISTORY OF QUARANTINE

The practice of quarantine began during the fourteenth century as an attempt to protect coastal cities from epidemics of plague and other infectious diseases, particularly from the East. Ships arriving in Venice, Italy, and ports along the Adriatic Sea were required to sit at anchor for 40 days before they were allowed to land. The isolation of ships, including passengers and goods, was a mandatory procedure. This practice, called "quarantine," was derived from the Latin word *quaresma*, meaning "40."

When the United States first gained its independence from Great Britain in the late 1700s, little was done to prevent the importation of infectious diseases. Although some attempts were made to impose quarantine requirements, protections against imported diseases were considered a local matter and handled by the individual states. It was because of severe yellow fever epidemics that Congress finally passed the Federal Quarantine Legislation in 1878.

Today, the Division of Global Migration and Quarantine is part of the CDC's National Center for Preparedness, Detection, and Control of Infectious Diseases and is headquartered in Atlanta, Georgia. Quarantine stations are located in Atlanta, Chicago, Honolulu, Los Angeles, Miami, New York, San Francisco, and Seattle. Quarantine operations involve the cooperation of several agencies, including state and local health agencies, Customs and Border Protection, the U.S. Department of Agriculture (USDA), and the Bureau of Citizenship and Immigration Services.

tion of suspected SARS cases is mandatory. How long patients should remain in isolation depends on whether and to what extent they continue to shed the virus from their respiratory tract or feces after obvious clinical symptoms such as coughing have stopped. Currently, at least 14 days of home quarantine are recommended after a suspected SARS patient is discharged from the hospital.

HAND WASHING AS A PREVENTIVE MEASURE

Hand washing is a preventive measure against the spread of SARS, as it is against most infectious diseases. Several epidemiological studies confirmed the effectiveness of hand washing as a measure against disease transmission in institutional and community settings. The studies suggested that hand washing was protective against the virus when comparing infected cases and noninfected cases. More conclusive studies are necessary to make it a definitive finding so the information can be widely disseminated. Nevertheless, good common sense and old public health strategies such as hand washing have worked against the transmission of infectious diseases in the past and are still relied on today.

RESPONDING TO A HEALTH CRISIS

Courageous health care workers around the world, particularly nurses and doctors, were infected, became ill, and even died caring for patients with SARS during the 2003 outbreak. Responding to the health crisis of the highly contagious coronavirus, they put their lives on the line in their role as health care providers. They quickly separated SARS patients from their families and other hospital patients to diminish the risk of infection. In addition, health workers had to wear uncomfortable equipment to protect themselves, which made their working conditions more trying. They worked tirelessly to recognize SARS patients and isolate them, since early detection was critical to minimize the outbreak.

The most significant measure to keep the SARS epidemic from spreading further was the implementation of the old practice of quarantine, which prevented the epidemic from becoming more widely spread.

The World Health Organization issued an unprecedented travel advisory during the 2003 outbreak, warning people not to travel to China, Vietnam, Taiwan, Hong Kong, and Toronto unless absolutely necessary in order to minimize the export of the disease to other countries. Moreover, governments built emergency response teams using networks of staff and financial resources, while scientists raced to break the genetic code of the SARS virus to find effective treatments.

4

Diagnosis and Management of SARS

The clinical diagnosis of SARS remains based on epidemiological background, clinical manifestations, and differentiation of the disease from other infections. The epidemiological portion of the diagnosis looks for possible avenues through which the disease might have spread—for example, if the patient traveled to China or danced with a known SARS patient. Lack of reliable, standardized tests for SARS virus antibody detection made diagnosis difficult, to say the least. Recently, reliable tests and methods have been adequately field tested, diagnosis will continue to be arduous and lengthy for doctors.

Two types of laboratory test are becoming available. One is a molecular (PCR) test, which can detect genetic material of the SARS-CoV in various specimens, such as blood, stool, and respiratory secretions. The other type of test detects antibodies produced in response to the SARS-CoV infection. Different types of antibodies (IgM and IgG) appear and change in level during the course of the infection.

Humans have an immune system to protect them from the negative consequences of infections. As mentioned earlier, antibodies are small proteins that the human body develops to counter the presence of foreign organisms such as viruses or bacteria. Natural immunity is acquired when a patient has a disease and recovers from it. For example, if you have had the measles, you are not likely to contract it again because your body has produced antibodies to protect you against the measles virus. These antibodies often provide protection for the rest of your life. Vaccines provide the same protection, but with the benefit of not having to experience the disease. A vaccine injects a weakened or killed pathogen into the body—usually not enough to cause disease symptoms, but enough to start an immune response that will produce antibodies to fight the disease, should it ever confront or challenge the body again.

RISK FACTORS

SARS is very contagious. People with SARS are most likely infectious when they have symptoms of the disease such as fever and cough. It is not known for how long they are infectious before their symptoms begin, or how infectious they may be. There are risk factors that can increase the probability that someone will contract the disease. People at a higher risk, as previously mentioned, include older persons with chronic conditions and health care workers who have direct contact with SARS patients.

A person may be at greater risk if he or she has cared for, lived with, or been in direct contact with the respiratory secretions and/or body fluids of a person suspected of having SARS. In the case of health workers, they have to take precautionary measures and follow specific SARS care guidelines. The Centers for Disease Control and Prevention (CDC) as well as the Canadian Health Authorities developed recommendations to prevent the transmission of respiratory pathogens to health care workers as they perform procedures that carry the risk of transmitting infection from the ill patient. When caring for SARS patients, health care workers are urged to

- Use gloves.

- Wear an N95 mask (a special mask that covers the nose and mouth and is designed to filter the air before the person wearing the mask inhales, to keep out any pathogens that may be carried through the air).

- Use eye protection.

- Wear gowns.

- Follow scrupulous hand hygiene (washing with both soap and alcohol).

Also, the above protective materials must be properly discarded and replaced (if necessary) before the health care worker visits another patient.

The rapid spread of SARS among health care workers in Hanoi, Vietnam, and in hospitals in Hong Kong confirmed the potentially highly contagious nature of the SARS virus. Medical personnel, physicians, nurses, and hospital workers were among those commonly infected. Attack rates in excess of 50 percent have been reported among health workers who treated SARS patients. SARS infection of health care workers is probably related to increased contact with respiratory secretions, contact with patients during the most contagious phase of the illness, and/or contact with particular patients who have an increased likelihood (for instance, due to other diseases) of spreading SARS.

Diagnostic and therapeutic procedures inside the hospital, such as diagnostic sputum induction, bronchoscopy, endotracheal intubation, and airway suction are potent aerosol-generating procedures and are now recognized as high-risk activities for hospital personnel and visitors.

Obviously, hospital workers must use precautions. But SARS can still occur despite knowledge about epidemiology and transmission of the virus. To reduce the number of unrecognized cases, the Singapore Ministry of Health recommended a strategy to quickly identify **febrile** (having a high fever) or symptomatic persons with chronic illnesses or any recent health care facility contact as a suspected case for isolation. Following strict isolation procedures is very important in decreasing the spread of SARS.

There is no indication that SARS can spread widely through a community, since in most cases close contact has to occur to assist the spread of the disease. Therefore, when patients with SARS are identified and placed in quarantine, strict isolation should be observed. The report of three family members of a SARS patient who became infected during a hospital quarantine that was not observed properly was a costly lesson in how strictly isolation measures must be carried out when dealing with SARS. Patients diagnosed with SARS may or may not actually be infected with

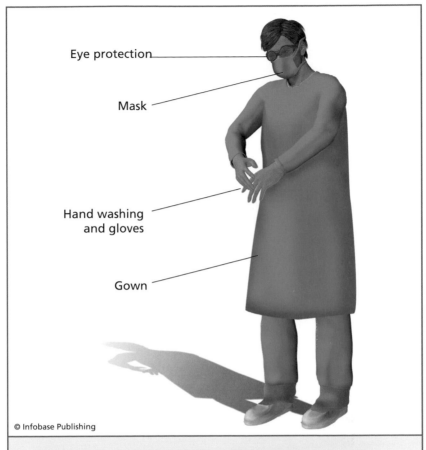

Eye protection

Mask

Hand washing
and gloves

Gown

© Infobase Publishing

Figure 4.1 At the height of the SARS outbreak, many people tried to take every possible precaution to avoid contracting the disease. Although the wearing of safety gear, as shown in this illustration, was recommended only for those at high risk of infection, such as hospital workers, ordinary people were often seen wearing surgical masks and gloves while going about their daily business.

the SARS virus, but even if they are not infected, they are at risk of contracting the disease if they are housed with infected patients.

Health care facilities should emphasize the importance of infection control measures for all respiratory infections, and if there is a good reason for doctors and the health department to

DO SURGICAL MASKS STOP SARS?

The dramatic photos of people walking the streets of Asian cities wearing surgical masks suggest that these masks might be a good prophylactic and protection against the disease.

Although the CDC does advise people who have SARS to wear these masks, they do not recommend them for people in contact with those patients unless the infected person can't wear one him- or herself. Wearing surgical masks outdoors, where virus-laden particles easily disperse, even through the fabric of the mask, has even less value.

The CDC does advise health care workers involved with SARS patients to wear a special mask called an N95 respirator. But even these masks offer limited protection from coronaviruses. The "95" in the name of the device means that, if the mask is properly fitted, it can filter particles as small as 0.3 microns 95 percent of the time. Human coronaviruses measure between 0.1 and 0.2 nitrons, which is one to two times smaller than the cutoff size. Properly fitted, the N95 mask seems to offer better protection than nothing, but is not a guarantee that the wearer will not become infected with SARS.

To efficiently protect yourself against coronaviruses, you would need to wear a full-faced mask with a high-efficiency particle air filter.

suspect a person might have SARS, then the patient should immediately be placed on SARS isolation precautions, and all contacts with the ill patient should be identified, evaluated, and monitored for signs of infection.

Additionally, extreme caution has to be taken in the handling and consumption of exotic animals in parts of the world where such creatures are considered culinary delicacies. As you will recall, SARS-CoV was found in three animal species taken from a market in southern China (masked palm civet, raccoon dog, and Chinese ferret badger). Antibody studies in people working in markets that sell these animals show that they have a higher **prevalence** of antibodies to SARS-CoV in comparison with the general population. As a precautionary measure, persons who might come into contact with these species or their products, including body fluids and excretions, should be aware of the possible health risks, mostly during close contact such as handling and slaughtering, and possibly also food processing and consumption.

Another risk to be avoided is traveling to countries with active SARS outbreaks. The areas that had the greatest number of SARS cases include China, Singapore, Canada (the Toronto area), and Vietnam.

TESTING FOR THE SARS VIRUS

Since the 2003 SARS outbreak, virologists and epidemiologists have not been idle. They have unlocked a partial genome of this coronavirus, based on a sequence of the SARS coronavirus replicase gene. The **polymerase chain reaction (PCR)** technique is a test that can detect viral genetic material; in SARS patients, it can identify the SARS-CoV in tissue samples from patients.

Now that doctors know what viral material to look for in possible SARS cases, presence of the virus can be confirmed more rapidly, instead of administering several tests, as was needed when SARS was first discovered. Tests for the virus can be done on samples taken from the respiratory tract, the feces, and the urine. Evidence of SARS viral replication has also been found in the gastrointestinal tract, which suggests that the SARS virus is not just confined to the lung. This finding confirmed speculation that SARS can be spread not only by the respiratory route, but also by the fecal route.

Epidemiological findings showing lower transmission rates in the early course of infection were reinforced by lab findings of poor RT-PCR assay results during the early course of the infections. However, viral RNA may be detected by RT-PCR for months after the onset of disease. Rapid detection by nucleic acid amplification such as RT-PCR or antigen detection are the best techniques of virus identification.

It has been determined that because of the **genomic** organization of SARS coronavirus, that all mRNA molecules contain the nucleocapsid gene sequence region of the SARS coronavirus. Therefore, targeting this nucleocapsid gene sequence will increase diagnostic sensitivity.

Quantitative RT-PCR of a nasopharyngeal aspirate is the most sensitive and rapid method for aiding in clinical diagnosis and may achieve a **sensitivity** (the percentage of people with disease found positive by the test) of 80 percent with good specificity even if it is collected within the first five days of illness.

Stool specimens should also be routinely sent for testing since a very high percentage of patients develop diarrhea and shed the virus during the second week of illness. Lastly, antigen detection with monoclonal antibodies is also a sensitive and specific test for diagnosis of SARS. Antibody tests detect antibodies produced in response to the SARS coronavirus infection. Different types of antibodies appear and change in levels during the course of infection. As serum antibody levels start to rise at day seven, more than 80 percent of SARS cases can be detected within the first days after the onset of the disease. For antibody testing, the indirect immunofluorescent antibody test is more commonly used than the neutralizing antibody test since the former involves minimal manipulation of infectious virus and therefore carries less risk of a biohazard.

Isolating the SARS virus is another test that can be done to indicate the presence of live SARS-CoV. The virus can be detected by inoculating suitable cell cultures with patients' cultures (such as respiratory secretion, blood, or stool) and growing the virus *in vitro* (outside the body; often referring to the laboratory setting). Once isolated, the virus must be identified as SARS-CoV through further tests. If the cell culture results indicate that SARS is present in the sample tested, the patient is diagnosed with SARS. However, negative cell culture results do not necessarily mean that the person does not have SARS, because, as previously stated, the test is not 100 percent accurate in identifying all cases, especially early ones in which the patient may have a low viral load.

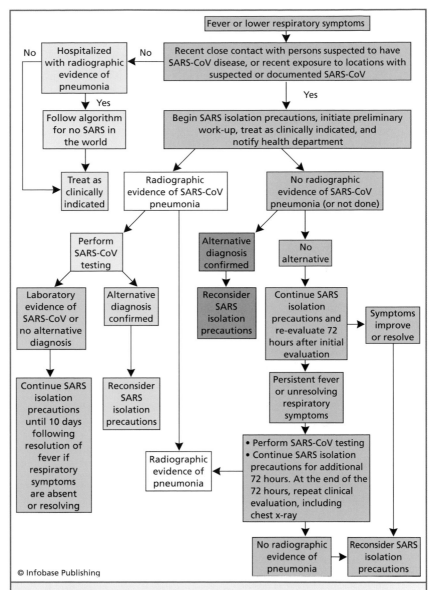

Figure 4.2 The efficient cooperation among global health agencies helped stop the spread of SARS before it could kill hundreds of thousands or even millions, and put into place procedures to follow when dealing with suspected SARS cases. This chart shows steps that medical professionals are supposed to follow when they are trying to determine whether a patient who shows a fever or lower respiratory symptoms (see top of chart) may, in fact, have SARS.

DIAGNOSIS

The diagnosis of SARS-CoV disease and the implementation of control measures should be based on the degree of the patient's risk of exposure. According to CDC guidelines, in the absence of any person-to-person transmission of SARS-CoV worldwide, the overall likelihood that a patient being evaluated for fever or respiratory illness has SARS will be exceedingly low unless there are both typical clinical findings and some additional epidemiological evidence that raises suspicion that the person has been exposed to SARS-CoV. Perhaps, only patients who require hospitalization for unexplained pneumonia and who have an epidemiological history that raises the suspicion of SARS exposure, such as recent travel to a known SARS-affected area or close contact with an ill person with such a travel history, should even be considered for a SARS diagnosis. Suspicions should also arise when health workers who have had direct patient contact, a technician in a laboratory that works with live SARS-CoV, or someone with an epidemiological link to a cluster of cases of unexplained pneumonia shows the symptoms typical of SARS. Figure 4.2 on the previous page illustrates the algorithm (instructions) for evaluation and management of patients who are hospitalized for X-ray–confirmed pneumonia.

CONFIRMING THE DIAGNOSIS

To confirm a SARS diagnosis, several tests have to be performed. A complete blood test is necessary because, during the course of illness, abnormal blood values are common. **Lymphopenia** (an abnormal lowering of the blood's lymphocyte count, a type of white cell) and **thrombocytopenia** (an abnormally low number of thrombocytes, or platelets) are frequent. Transient **leukopenia** (an abnormal reduction in the number of all white blood cells) is also found in patients during their first weeks of illness. In addition, a great number of patients also have low calcium, phosphorus, magnesium, sodium, and potassium levels. Elevated levels of lactate dehydrogenase and aspartate

Figure 4.3 Once the virus that is responsible for causing SARS was identified and isolated, it became easier
to determine whether a particular person was suffering
from SARS or from some other respiratory illness. Before
making a definitive diagnosis of SARS, health care professionals must take samples of blood, sputum, or other
bodily fluids from the patient and subject them to many
tests to confirm that the SARS virus is present. Test
strips like this one will show a color change to indicate
whether the virus is present. (© Deanne Fitzmaurice/
San Francisco Chronicle/Corbis)

have also been mentioned in studies, and these levels are used to help further confirm a SARS infection. It remains unclear whether these abnormalities reflect the natural course of the SARS infection or whether they occur because of the effects of treatment with agents that influence renal function—that is, the kidney's ability to do its job.

Additional tests to help confirm a diagnosis of possible SARS cases are necessary. For example, chest X-rays are used to identify pneumonia. Influenza tests and blood cultures are needed to eliminate the possibility that the illness is being caused by other microorganisms. All parameters involved in the diagnosis are important. In the case of SARS, both the clinical examination and the radiological and laboratory tests are of the utmost importance, as is a travel history and history of contact with possible SARS cases.

SARS CASE DEFINITION

To classify patients with unexplained pneumonia that raise a suspicion of SARS, the World Health Organization has come out with guidelines for a SARS case definition.

As defined by the World Health Organization, there are currently two SARS classification categories: suspected cases and probable cases.

A *suspected case* is classified as a disease in a person

- with a documented fever (temperature greater than 98.6°F/38°C);

- lower respiratory tract symptoms, such as pneumonia;

- close contact with a person believed to have had SARS during the ten days prior to the onset of symptoms; or

- a history of travel to a geographic area where there has been documented transmission of the illness.

A *probable case* is a suspected case with

- chest X-ray findings of pneumonia;

- acute respiratory distress syndrome (RDS); or

- an unexplained respiratory illness resulting in death with autopsy findings that seem to show the person had RDS without an identifiable cause.

The CDC has added laboratory criteria for evidence of infection with SARS-CoV to its current surveillance case definition. Using these criteria, a SARS case is considered laboratory-confirmed if one of the following criteria is met:

- detection of antibodies to SARS-associated coronavirus in a serum sample;

- detection of SARS-CoV RNA by RT-PCR confirmed by a second PCR (polymerase chain reaction) assay, by using a second sample of the specimen and a different set of PCR primers; or

- isolation of SARS-CoV in culture.

Negative laboratory results for PCR, viral culture, or antibody tests obtained within 28 days of illness do not rule out a coronavirus infection, perhaps even the coronavirus that causes SARS.

PROBLEMS WITH SARS TESTING

All tests for SARS-CoV that are available at this time have some limitations. Extreme caution is therefore necessary when patient management decisions must be based on virological test results. SARS-CoV testing should be considered if no alternative diagnosis is made within 72 hours after the clinical evaluation has begun and the patient is thought to be at high risk for SARS. Health care providers should immediately report all positive SARS-CoV test results to the local or state health department. Testing to confirm a SARS diagnosis at an appropriate test site should be arranged through the local or state health department.

5

Treatment of SARS

Prevention and control of SARS-CoV transmission in the community are still the most effective ways to stop this often-fatal infectious disease. Prevention and control rely on prompt identification and management of both SARS patients and their contacts. This approach has so far proven to be the best treatment, due to the absence of a specific SARS vaccine or a definitive treatment. When a vaccine or effective antiviral agent become available in the future, they will, naturally, become the treatment and prevention options of choice. Advances in vaccine development and effective treatments are discussed in this chapter.

MANAGING SARS

Countries that face SARS outbreaks have implemented classic public health measures, including case detection, isolation, infection control, and contact tracing to successfully treat the epidemic. In addition, population screening for the early detection of SARS, with the use of a tool as simple as a thermometer, supported by mass public education and information campaigns, were decisive in avoiding the further spread of the disease.

ISOLATION

Isolation refers to separating infected people from healthy people and restricting the infected patients' movement to stop the spread of the illness to otherwise healthy people. It is used for patients who are known to have the SARS illness. Isolation allows for the focused delivery of specialized health care to people who are ill, and it protects healthy people from getting sick. People in isolation may be cared for in their homes, in hospitals, or in specially designated health care facilities.

Figure 5.1 Despite scientific evidence that surgical masks are ineffective at preventing the spread of airborne particles of the SARS virus, many people regularly wore masks in public during the height of the SARS epidemic, particularly in Asia, where the most infections occurred. (AP Images)

QUARANTINE

Quarantine, like isolation, is also intended to stop the spread of SARS. Quarantine is used for people who have been exposed to the virus but who may or may not become ill. In quarantine situations, the person who has been exposed, though not yet ill, is separated from other people and kept in a restricted area, because he or she may still become infectious. During the 2003 global SARS outbreak, patients in the United States were quarantined until they were no longer infectious. This practice allowed patients to receive appropriate care, and it helped contain the spread of the illness. Seriously ill patients were cared for in hospitals, while persons with mild illness were cared for at home. Those being cared for at home were asked to avoid contact with other people and to remain at home until ten days after any fever and respiratory symptoms had fully gone away.

MEDICATIONS

In addition to controlling the spread of SARS, when confronted with specific SARS cases, doctors have a wide range

THE DISCOVERY OF ANTIBIOTICS

The success of antibiotics in attacking bacteria can be considered one of modern medicine's greatest achievements. First used frequently during World War II (1939–1945), antibiotics have saved many lives and reduced or even eliminated some complications of long-feared diseases and infections.

During the late-nineteenth century, people began to accept the germ theory of disease, which stated that bacteria and other microorganisms were the cause of disease and illness. Scientists thus began to search for substances that could kill these "germs" and rid the body of the disease. One of the pioneers who showed that harmless bacteria could treat disease was Louis Pasteur. He demonstrated that the bacterial disease anthrax could be thwarted in animals by a simple injection of bacteria found in common soil. Following Pasteur's discovery, a German scientist by the name of E. de Freudenreich extracted a substance from a type of bacteria that was found to act as an antibiotic.

In 1928, the British scientist Alexander Fleming had a breakthrough. One night, he left some Petri dishes on which he had been growing *Staphylococcus* bacteria out in his laboratory. When he returned to the lab, he noticed that there were certain areas of the plate where no bacteria appeared. A cluster of blue-green mold called *Penicillium* was growing of medicines they can prescribe. To treat people already infected with the SARS virus, several treatments have been used with a certain degree of success. Nevertheless, the lack of an effective specific treatment for SARS has been frustrating, and the search for a safe and definitive treatment continues to be a major challenge for scientists even now that the SARS epidemic has been contained.

Figure 5.2 Alexander Fleming. (AP Images)

on the plate near the area where the bacteria were absent. Through additional research, Fleming was able to show that a chemical substance in the mold was lethal to *Staphylococcus* bacteria. This substance, once extracted from the mold, was named "penicillin" after the mold that led Fleming to his discovery.

Antibiotics

Among the first prescribed drugs used to try to treat SARS cases were **antibiotics**. However, SARS itself is caused by a virus and cannot be killed by antibiotics. Antibiotic therapy can be useful for SARS patients if they also contract a bacterial infection. In addition to their **antibacterial** effects, some antibiotics are known to have **immunomodulatory** properties, helping to regulate the immune system.

Antibiotics are relatively new drugs. The first anti-infective agents were the sulfa drugs developed around 1940. They were widely used for various infections, such as earaches. The penicillins, developed shortly thereafter, were considerably better at treating a broader spectrum of bacterial diseases. Derivatives of those early penicillins are still used today. Antibiotics are the only drugs that actually cure patients of bacterial illnesses. Other drugs just provide relief or control symptoms.

Antiviral Drugs

In addition to antibiotics, **antiviral** agents have also been prescribed from the outset of the SARS epidemic, despite lack of evidence about whether they are actually effective. With the discovery of the SARS-CoV as the pathogen that causes SARS, scientific research institutions worldwide have been vigorously attempting to develop a useful antiviral agent to treat the disease.

For example, the drug ribavirin was widely used as an empirical therapy for SARS because of its broad-spectrum antiviral activity against both DNA and RNA viruses. The use of ribavirin has brought about much criticism because its usefulness has not been proven and because it has considerable side effects. Side effects such as hemolytic anemia (low red blood cell count) and rises in transaminase (a liver enzyme that can potentially signal liver function problems when elevated) are dose-related. However, for dying patients, without proven treatment options, treatments that *might* work should be tried.

Corticosteroids

Another treatment commonly used for SARS patients is corticosteroids (synthetic, more powerful agents than the naturally occurring cortisone). Corticosteroids have been the mainstay of immunomodulatory therapy for SARS. Their timely use often led to early improvement in terms of making fever subside and improving the patient's ability to take in and use oxygen. However, there is much skepticism and controversy about the use of corticosteroids, centering on their degree of effectiveness, their potential negative effects (including the suppression of the immune system), and their impact on final patient outcomes. The timing of using corticosteroids for SARS patients should coincide with the onset of a truly excessive immune response; otherwise, the weakened immune system could actually make the patient's condition worse. The duration and dosage of corticosteroids also has to be closely monitored.

Herbal Remedies

In China, traditional herbal medicine has been frequently used in conjunction with Western medicine to treat SARS. Glycyrrhizin, which is derived from licorice roots, is sometimes believed to be effective against SARS when given in very high concentrations. Again, data from clinical trials about how well glycyrrhizin works are lacking. Therefore, no one can be certain at this point if the herb is really effective and, if it is, how exactly it works.

Interferons and Immunoglobulins

Lastly, doctors may treat SARS with human interferons and human immunoglobulins (an infusion of nonspecific antibodies). Human interferons are a family of **cytokines** important in the cellular immune response. Anecdotal studies have shown that patients recover faster when interferon is used in combination with immunoglobulins. Human immunoglobulins were used to treat SARS in some hospitals in China and

Hong Kong. Many times, these medicines were used in conjunction with corticosteroids. Their effectiveness in treating SARS remains uncertain at this stage.

SARS TREATMENT ADVANCES

Since the 2003 SARS outbreaks, research to develop efficacious treatments is a priority. Projects are geared toward finding or designing drugs to inhibit viral replication. Replication of SARS-CoV requires **proteases** (protein-digestive enzymes) that could be important targets for those potential antiviral drugs. During the last five years, developments have shown potential antiviral activity, but have not yet been evaluated in human models and only in a few animal ones. Antiviral activity has been shown in the following:

- Protease inhibitors such as nelfinavir and glycyrrhizin among others have been found to have antiviral activity in vitro.

- Antiviral peptides designed against the S protein also showed potential in vitro to inhibit membrane fusion and cell entry.

- Small interfering RNA also hold potential in reducing cytopathic effects, viral replication and viral protein expression in living cells.

These therapeutic advances are tools that may help to treat SARS patients in the future. The discovery of inhibitors against SARS 3C-like proteinase, which can be potentially optimized as drugs, is promising. The 3C-like proteinase is recognized as a potential drug design target for the treatment of SARS. Several studies showed very weak beneficial evidence of using Chinese herbs combined with Western medicines. The benefit appeared to be from a decrease in the dosage of corticosteroids. At the moment, no effective treatments or vaccines are yet proven effective and safe.

The most efficient treatments for SARS are the old, tried-and-true strategies such as isolation of infected patients.

Options to contain the spread of infections are still important in managing epidemics such as SARS. Prevention is the simplest and least costly strategy to contain SARS.

SARS VACCINE DEVELOPMENT

The development of effective and safe vaccines to prevent infection by the SARS coronavirus is needed since it can easily be grown in cell culture and rapidly spread from person to person. In addition, the virus is highly infectious. Since 2004 heat-inactivated virus vaccines have been used in China. There are, however, reservations regarding the efficacy and the long-term safety of this kind of vaccine. Concerns about the risk of infection of the workers producing the vaccines are legitimate during the handling of the processes.

Current research leading to the development of an effective and safe vaccine appears to be using a residue from the receptor binding portion of the S protein of the coronavirus. This will create antibody production in humans sufficient to prevent a full SARS infection after any future exposure. With the identification of SARS-CoV functional receptor and the mapping of the receptor-binding domain (RBD) on the S protein, it is possible to develop vaccines targeting the receptor binding.

The S protein of the SARS-CoV is a transmembrane glycoprotein that is responsible for virus binding, fusion, and cell entry of the virus; it is also a major inducer of neutralizing antibodies. The RBD of SARS-CoV S protein contains multiple epitopes capable of inducing highly potent neutralizing antibody response and protective immunity, and therefore it may serve as an important target site for developing SARS vaccines.

Since targeting the receptor-binding domain, it is now possible that antibodies specific for RBD will block binding of any virus to the target cell. Summarizing, once those neutralizing epitopes were identified, hopes rose that the inactivated virus

Racing to Find a SARS Vaccine

A vaccine that is created in 15 to 20 years is considered speedy, but scientists are hoping to create a vaccine for SARS much sooner than that.

Vaccine development

Research
Studies focus on the biological mechanisms of the organism that causes damage to the body.

Pre-clinical evaluations
Vaccine preparations are tested in cell cultures and lab animals. Computer models are sometimes used to visualize the vaccine and its interaction in the body.

Clinical trials
Hundreds of human volunteers are given the vaccine. They are frequently tested and evaluated over long periods of time to assess the safety and progress of the vaccine.

Approval
The Food and Drug Administration approves a vaccine after it is proven to be safe, effective in preventing disease, and remains stable and potent during its shelf life.

Traditional vaccines

Type	Description	Used to fight
Inactivated	Dead disease-causing bacteria or virus that stimulates a weak immune system response; must be given more than once.	Influenza, cholera, plague, and hepatitis A
Attenuated	Live, weakened version of a virus that is easy for the body to defend against. Usually given only once.	Yellow fever, mumps, measles and rubella

Second-generation vaccines

Type	Description	Used to fight
Conjugate	Parts of a second virus, easily recognized and defeated by the immune system, are linked to the outside of disease-causing bacteria or virus.	Haemophilus influenzae type b (Hib), a type of bacterial meningitis
Subunit	Antigenic fragments of the virus used to evoke an immune system response.	Pneumonia and hepatitis B
Recombinant vector	Harmless genetic material from a disease-causing organism is carried inside a weakened second virus.	Currently being tested for use against AIDS and hepatitis B*

* A combined recombinant subunit vaccine used.

Sources: Centers for Disease Control and Prevention, U.S. Department of Health and Human Services.
© Infobase Publishing

Figure 5.3 Ever since the discovery of the virus that causes SARS, scientists have raced to find an effective vaccine that will prevent people from contracting SARS in the first place. This chart shows the steps that commonly occur in the development of a new vaccine.

vaccines could be replaced by vaccines based on fragments containing neutralizing epitopes with the goal of blocking virus binding and fusion.

THE HISTORY OF VACCINES

Have you recently had your tetanus shot? What about the chicken pox vaccine? And although you probably do not remember, you received the measles, mumps, and rubella vaccines when you were a baby. These vaccines prevent you from getting a debilitating or potentially lethal disease. In fact, the smallpox vaccine is no longer given because, through its use, the disease has been completely eradicated. Today, vaccines exist for many diseases, and scientists are currently researching methods to defend against even more scourges.

The form of vaccine that we are familiar with is a relatively modern development, but the theory behind vaccines is much older. In the fifteenth century, the Chinese would deliberately infect themselves with material from smallpox blisters. By scraping some pus from a smallpox blister (pustule) and rubbing it on a scratch or small cut in their own skin, an uninfected person could induce a mild form of the disease. After the person had recovered, he or she was immune to smallpox. This technique was called *variolation*.

The concept of variolation eventually spread to England and caught the attention of a country doctor named Edward Jenner. Jenner noticed that dairymaids, who often contracted cowpox (a disease similar to, but not as deadly as, smallpox) did not contract smallpox. Jenner took the fluid from a cowpox pustule and placed it under the skin of a young boy. The young boy fell ill with cowpox, but quickly recovered. Shortly thereafter, Jenner infected the same boy with material from a smallpox pustule. The boy developed a blister at the site of infection but did not get sick. Jenner named his discovery *vaccination*, taking the name from the Latin word *vaca*, which means "cow." Vaccines have since been created to protect people from many diseases.

Phase I clinical trials of a DNA vaccine for SARS conducted by the National Institutes of Health (NIH) have shown hopeful results. The vaccine was well tolerated and induced neutralizing antibody responses in 80 percent of people vaccinated and T-cell immune responses in 100 percent of people vaccinated. Caution should prevail since these are results of Phase I trials, meaning the vaccine was tested only on 10 people, all of whom were healthy.[1] The results are nevertheless promising, and any vaccine efforts to eradicate SARS are commendable and necessary.

So far, the best way to avoid another epidemic remains prevention and control of SARS-CoV transmission within communities. Implementation of community containment measures rely on public trust. Community officials can generate public trust by communicating clear messages about the rationale for and the role and duration of community containment measures, and the ways in which affected persons will be supported.

6

Prevention and Public Health Measures

To contain the spread of a contagious illness, such as SARS, public health authorities rely on many strategies. Two of these strategies have already been explained: isolation and quarantine. Both strategies are partial treatment objectives. Both are common practices in public health, and both aim to control exposure to infected or potentially infected persons. Finally, both may be undertaken voluntarily or imposed by public health authorities. Isolation has been employed in the past to help control tuberculosis.

PUBLIC CONTROL OF SARS

Specific measures of prevention include national measures to contain SARS. The main focus of SARS surveillance activities in countries that have had no or very few SARS cases is on the early identification and isolation of patients who are suspected of having SARS. In contrast, countries that are affected by severe SARS outbreaks must immediately take a variety of sometimes unpopular measures to contain the epidemic. Generally, this is done by isolating patients and enforcing quarantine for suspected exposed patients. Other more drastic community measures guided toward containing the epidemic may also be established to prevent transmission from SARS patients, which is a critical component of controlling SARS.

Confirmed SARS patients should be admitted to a health care facility for isolation only if they have been clinically diagnosed or if isolation at home or in a community facility cannot be achieved safely and effectively. Home isolation is less disruptive to the patient's routine than isolation in a hospital or other community setting. Any patient's home that might be used as an isolation setting should be evaluated by the patient's physician or a local health department official to make sure it is suitable. The best homes for use as isolation centers would have a remotely located bedroom with its own attached bathroom, so that the patient can be completely removed from other family members. During the period of home isolation, household members who are not providing care to the patient should be relocated if possible, so that only the primary caregiver and the patient remain in the residence and vulnerable to the infection.

PREVENTING SARS AT HOME

Infection control measures in the home for both the patient and caregiver are very important to follow. Hand washing with soap and water and an alcohol-based hand rub are recommended after touching body fluids and contaminated surfaces such as bed linens. Towels and bedding should not be shared. These can be cleaned in a washing machine with regular detergent and hot water, but adding ordinary household bleach is also recommended as an extra measure of protection. Gloves and other protective attire are suggested. Patients should cover the nose and mouth when coughing and should dispose of tissues in a plastic-lined waste container. Patients should wear a surgical mask when other people are present. If patients cannot wear a mask for some reason, people who come in close contact with them should wear a mask instead. Use of disposable dishes and utensils during the duration of the isolation is also recommended.

For people who have been exposed to SARS patients, there should be a vigilant watch for fever and/or respiratory symptoms. People in the same household or other close contacts who show symptoms should follow the same precautions recommended for SARS patients.

PREVENTION METHODS FOR THE HEALTH CARE COMMUNITY

The CDC has also prepared guidelines for isolation and precaution for hospitals and health care facilities in the event that a SARS patient has to be admitted to a hospital. The goals for those health care facilities are to

- rapidly identify and isolate all potential SARS patients;

- implement infection control practices;

- trace all contacts to interrupt the spread of SARS-CoV;

- ensure rapid communication within individual health care facilities; and

- keep communication strong between different health care facilities and health departments.

BREAKING THE CHAIN OF TRANSMISSION

The goal for infection control in health care settings, homes, and communities is to recognize patients who are at risk of SARS-CoV disease as early as possible and to prevent the spread of SARS by implementing infection control precautions. In almost all documented cases, transmission of SARS appears to occur through close contact with infected persons. The most effective way to control SARS is to break the chain of transmission from infected to healthy persons. This requires limiting the public interactions of possible or known SARS patients, even if this is unpopular.

Preventing transmission of SARS through the use of a variety of community containment strategies to maximize success are very important in any public health initiative. Decisions to institute broader community measures take into

THE CENTERS FOR DISEASE CONTROL AND PREVENTION (CDC)

The mission of the Centers for Disease Control and Prevention (CDC) is to protect the health and safety of people both at home and abroad by providing information and collecting data on health, wellness, and disease.

The CDC, which has its main headquarters in Atlanta, Georgia, was organized in 1946 as a branch of the Public Health Service to provide practical help regarding communicable diseases. In the mid-1950s, when polio appeared in children who had received the recently approved Salk vaccine, the CDC investigated the problem and the national inoculation program was stopped. The cases of polio were traced to a contaminated vaccine obtained from a laboratory in California; the problem was corrected, and the inoculation program was resumed. A couple of years later, the CDC again used surveillance to trace the course of a massive influenza epidemic. From the data it gathered in 1957 and subsequent years, the CDC developed national guidelines for influenza vaccine.

As an agency of the Department of Health and Human Services, the CDC's mission is to promote health and quality of life by preventing and controlling disease, injury, and disability. To accomplish its goals, the CDC works with partners in the nation and all over the world to monitor health, detect and investigate health problems, conduct research to enhance disease prevention, develop and advocate sound public health policies, implement prevention strategies, promote healthy behaviors, foster safe and healthful environments, and provide leadership and training.

The CDC alone cannot protect the health of the American people. However, by engaging with others—from state and local health departments to private corporations, from media outlets to the general public—the agency can achieve its vision of a better, safer, and healthier world.

Figure 6.1 Some of the public health measures implemented to try to stop the spread of SARS were not very popular among local communities. Quarantine and isolation, for example, caused panic in some places, and led to a degree of discrimination against people who came down with SARS. Even less popular were programs in Asia that sprayed germ-killing chemicals in the air, in the hope of killing airborne SARS viruses (as the man in the blue smock is doing in this photograph). (AP Images)

consideration the epidemiological characteristics of the SARS outbreak, the health care resources available, and the level of community cooperation.

THE NEED FOR NEWS ABOUT SARS

Implementation of all community containment measures relies on public trust. Community officials can help gain public trust by making clear why and how long community containment measures such as quarantines will be in effect.

Nevertheless, there is a balance to be strived for: getting people to show enough concern to follow the necessary guidelines and to report possible suspicious events, but not enough to cause a widespread public panic or a sense of overwhelming hopelessness.

7

Impact and Significance of SARS

The impact of SARS on individuals and communities is monumental; from emotional fear, worry, anxiety, shame, guilt over infecting others, concerns about being a burden, blame, and even helplessness, to mass hysteria, social isolation, and discrimination against infected persons and their families. SARS is a new disease that alienates, causes isolation, introduces fear, reinforces discrimination and prejudices, removes one's sense of security, disrupts community mental health, and ultimately has threatened political and economic stability in Asian cities such as Singapore, Beijing, Taipei, and Hong Kong. Within just one week in 2003, it made Toronto—formerly a trendy tourist spot—a destination to avoid, at least for a time.

ECONOMIC EFFECTS OF SARS

The considerable economic impact of SARS illustrates the importance that a severe new disease can have in our closely interdependent and highly mobile global community. Published economic costs of the SARS outbreak of 2003, largely based on losses from canceled travel plans and decreased investment in Asia, range from $30 billion to $140 billion. In most of the severely affected areas, service industries and airlines suffered the greatest losses. Internationally, a number of trade events excluded participants from Hong Kong and other affected areas.

EFFECTS ON TRAVEL AND TOURISM

SARS and travel are interlinked. Travelers infected in early stages of the outbreak became vectors of the disease, and tourism and its industry

Figure 7.1 This photograph of a newly married Asian couple kissing through surgical masks during the height of the SARS outbreak is a poignant example of how the disease caused widespread fear and even what might be considered irrational behavior in those touched by the epidemic. (Reuters/Corbis)

became a victim of SARS, subsequently. As a consequence of the outbreak, many Asian manufacturers lost important opportunities to promote their products in major trade shows around the world. Cutbacks on flights and ship arrivals had a significant impact on the supply chain of Asian products. SARS also caused a major dip in Asian tourism.

During the 2003 SARS epidemic, travel restrictions were imposed to prevent the spread of SARS along the routes of international air travel. Travel-related recommendations, even postponing trips, were an important component of the global containment strategy. The objective for governments and local authorities was to collaborate in bringing the outbreak under control. Recommendations concerning travel were ended when epidemiological criteria indicating that

TRAVEL RESTRICTIONS AS A MEASURE TO CONTROL SARS

In coordinating the international response to SARS, the World Health Organization's overriding objective was to prevent SARS from becoming established as a pandemic (worldwide epidemic) disease. Sealing off opportunities for further international spread was a key strategy. As SARS spread along the routes of international air travel, travel-related recommendations were an important component of the global containment strategy.

Although there are no longer any SARS-related travel restrictions in place, it is always best to take precautions before you travel. For example, to help to protect yourself from infection, wash your hands thoroughly and often. Scrub well with soap or use an alcohol-based hand rub. In China, try not to visit food markets and avoid wildlife that is sold in these markets. Finally, learn as much as you can about the status of the countries you will be visiting. You can find information about disease outbreaks on the Centers for Disease Control and Prevention and World Health Organization's Web sites.

there was no longer a high risk to travelers were met. Although there are no SARS-related travel restrictions in place today, it is always wise to heed safety recommendations when you travel to make sure you enjoy a safe trip.

The World Travel and Tourism Council prepared estimates of the impact of SARS in the Asian region. It estimated that overall Asian employment faced a decline of between 12 and 41 percent. Negative impacts on Gross National Product (GNP) and other economic indicators in Asian countries do not capture the full social impact from job losses and company failures in the region. Losses in the tourism industry have repercussions on jobs and growth in other economic sectors. The negative economic impact will continue to be felt for some time, as the number of trips made by foreigners to affected areas in Asia may remain low for years. Officials in those areas are aware that the media need to be kept informed of the measures being taken to enhance travelers' security to gain the confidence of the world community.

Another example of the interconnectedness and interdependent nature of our world are the fears expressed in the business press of how supplies of parts for cars, cameras, video gear, and other product components from China could cause production shortfalls in key industries because thousands of workers were at home, ill, or had their factories shut down in Southeast Asia.

THE MEDIA AND PUBLIC PANIC

The media's focus on the virus informed the world and inspired immense international cooperation on research and implementation of control measures such as quarantine and isolation. On the other hand, the media's coverage exaggerated public fear, increasing the growing stigma attached to the illness. As a consequence, Chinese neighborhoods were deserted, recovering SARS patients were turned down for

jobs, and universities, even in the United States, made it difficult for Asian students to invite their families from back home
to attend commencement ceremonies.

Media coverage is only one of many elements of the international response. The World Health Organization (WHO)
and the Centers for Disease Control and Prevention (CDC)
were also responsible for containing the virus. The WHO's
activist stance incited a rapid response from countries like
Vietnam, which quickly helped curtail the virus's spread.
Similarly, the CDC worked closely with airlines, immigration
agencies, and airport authorities in the United States and
around the world to establish an excellent surveillance system
for the disease. This system was the key element in preventing
any major SARS outbreaks in the United States. The surveillance cooperation would have spotted any local clusters of
infection before they could spread to affect large numbers of
people.

SARS caused considerable social disruption and public
anxiety, even in areas well beyond the outbreak sites. Avoid-
ance of travel to certain areas was disproportionate to the
risk, as was the widespread wearing of surgical masks. The
psychological impact of SARS on health care workers, affected
individuals, their families, and the broader community has
not yet been fully evaluated. However, public awareness
about SARS had benefited society and all of us in terms of
persuading the general public to check frequently for fever
and report symptoms promptly. These actions generally
reduced the time between onset of symptoms and isolation
of patients, thus limiting opportunities for further exposures
and transmission.

HOW SARS WAS STOPPED

The significance of SARS as a public health threat is enor-
mous. All new infectious diseases are poorly understood, at

least in the beginning of epidemics, and are often associated with high mortality rates. SARS passed readily from person to person, requiring no vector; had no particular geographical affinity; mimicked the symptoms of many other, more mild diseases; took its heaviest toll on hospital workers; and spread internationally with alarming ease. The fact that SARS was contained just a few months after the first global alert, despite the absence of a vaccine, effective treatment, or a reliable diagnostic test, is a great success story for public health. It is also evidence of the willingness of the international community to form a united front against a shared threat.

SARS stimulated an emergency response and a level of media attention on a scale that may have changed public and political perceptions of the risks associated with emerging and epidemic-prone diseases. Reports in scientific publications and the media and from government agencies in several countries agree that SARS raised the profile of public health by demonstrating the severe adverse effects that a health problem can have on economic and social stability, as well as political situations.

WHO is continuing to build on the international networks of real-time collaboration that are improving our understanding of SARS and that helped identify its causative agent early in the outbreak. WHO has also posted guidelines for alert, verification, and public health management of SARS during the post-outbreak period on its Web site.

In local areas, health providers and state or local health departments follow guidelines developed by international agencies, cooperate fully, and share information for the well-being of the individual patient as well as the whole community.

GLOBAL AND INDIVIDUAL EFFORTS TO STOP SARS
The reaction to SARS has been a good example of what is possible when health authorities and health care workers

participate cooperatively toward a common goal of education, prevention, and rapid control and treatment of an infectious disease.

A great deal of effort is now being expended on the development of a specific diagnostic test that will be able to tell SARS apart from other respiratory infections. As you might imagine, making a definitive diagnosis sooner would lead to earlier control activities, which should reduce the number of cases in any community. As physicians acquire more experience with SARS and become more familiar with its symptoms, better diagnostic accuracy may be expected.

There is also a lot of work continuing toward the development of a SARS virus vaccine. Vaccination against viral diseases is an integral part of worldwide communicable disease control. Vaccines against SARS will not only reduce the incidence of the disease, but will also decrease the social and economic burden of the disease on communities and individuals. Illness takes a devastating toll on the patients themselves as well as their communities. Families receive less income when a wage earner cannot work, and when caregivers must also stay home, additional wages are lost. Taken all together, these losses harm tax revenues, industrial production, and the wealth of communities around the world.

In cases where a person contracts a communicable disease such as SARS and has not been immunized, the use of drugs to control the severity of the disease as well as its symptoms becomes extremely important. Effective drugs will likely play a big role in the control and treatment of SARS in coming decades.

The future will surely bring effective and specific vaccines for SARS as well as medications that will decrease symptoms, speed recovery, and perhaps even cure the disease once it starts an infection. When this happens, past experience tells us to be watchful, because people tend to let their guard down when drugs or vaccines become available. We often forget about the dangers of infectious disease and become careless. If this ever happens in regard to SARS, it will be necessary for us to renew our commitment to early identification and treatment.

8

Lessons Learned from the SARS Epidemic

By the mid-twentieth century many infectious diseases were on the verge of being eradicated, at least in the Western world, due to the discovery and use of antibiotics, better sanitary conditions, better nutrition, and preventive measures against infectious diseases such as vaccinations. Control of infectious diseases became elusive however, when diseases thought to have been eradicated, such as malaria and tuberculosis, made a comeback in the late-twentieth century. In addition to the reemergence of these diseases, new (emerging) diseases such as acquired immunodeficiency syndrome (AIDS), severe acute respiratory syndrome (SARS), Ebola, and avian flu have also appeared. In an age when global travel allows businesspeople and tourists to visit far-flung countries, workers to migrate in search of better economic opportunities, and when people are displaced due to wars and political conflicts, the emergence and reemergence of infectious diseases are a real threat for global health.

It is an illusion that infectious diseases are mostly prevalent in underdeveloped countries. With the mobility of people in the twenty-first century, the risks of disease spreading globally are higher. No country is immune to epidemics; the SARS epidemic in 2003 is a good example. Infectious diseases are the world's number-one killer, and since the late 1980s, the death rate from infectious diseases has increased 58 percent in the United States alone.[1] Infectious diseases such as HIV/AIDS, tuberculosis, malaria, and diarrheal diseases account for approximately one-quarter of all deaths in the world. Since 2001, the United Sates has improved its

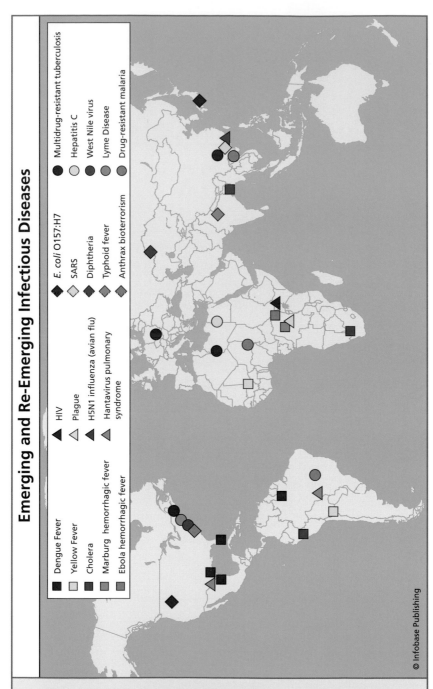

Figure 8.1 New and old infectious diseases periodically emerge and reemerge in epidemics around the world.

strategies to prepare for acts of bioterrorism, in which deadly microorganisms are used to threaten national security.

Emerging infectious diseases, because they are caused by new pathogens, spread rapidly through populations, since there is no natural immunity yet. Reemerging diseases are already known pathogens that reappear after a decline in incidence. SARS is an example of an emerging infection. It was caused by a previously unknown coronavirus. The first case of human SARS occurred in the Guangdong province of China; the virus spread through the slaughter of infected animals in crowded markets.

The SARS outbreak is a model study for infectious disease epidemiology. The infectious source and the disease host were identified and the path of its spread through Asia, and later Canada, was able to be followed. Further, containment policies using public health measures such as quarantine and prevention were essential to control SARS. However, SARS can reemerge due to adaptation, which is the mutation of new strains of the SARS coronavirus. In summary, SARS was controlled because of quick public health actions, international intervention, and cooperation through the mobilization of national governments and health authorities. Early reporting of outbreaks are of paramount importance in order to prevent future epidemic threats, such as those inflicted by the SARS or the avian influenza virus.

Reemerging diseases are those which have been around for a long time and return at various times or locations. For example, the West Nile virus, which existed in Africa and the Middle East for centuries, reemerged in Queens, New York, by an unknown route in 1999. Since then, the infection has spread westward across the United States.

Emerging and reemerging infectious diseases put pressure on medical communities and governments to control the dissemination of epidemics by identifying and controlling reservoirs, cooperating in prevention, and finding effective treatments and vaccines.

We can never be certain where or when the next outbreak of an emerging or reemerging infection might take place.

Infectious disease specialists worry about the combining of viruses in patients who might have a common respiratory or stomach flu and then come in contact with a deadly virus in which the viral proteins from the two viruses combine to form a new virus.

THE THREAT OF GLOBAL EPIDEMICS

In addition to the deaths that the SARS outbreak caused, it sounded a warning of the other major epidemics that could arise. In today's world epidemics have the potential of rapidly becoming global threats since they do not recognize political or national boundaries.

In fact, epidemics can show us just how meaningless these barriers are. For example, the People's Republic of China and Taiwan have no formal diplomatic relations, yet, being near each other, their experiences can help their people if their governments were to communicate.

With this in mind, people who are against sending aid to other countries might want to rethink their stance. For example, if a polio outbreak in Mexico gets out of control, the chances are good that polio will spread into the United States, as well as to other places. Helping Mexican health authorities stop the disease at its original site is far cheaper, safer, and more efficient than waiting for it to spread.

The experience of controlling the SARS-CoV virus provided some lessons on how to prepare for major outbreaks in the future. Improving overall preparedness and general infection control procedures are measures that are commonsense and will improve the ability to manage the next epidemic, because the question is not *if* there will be a future epidemic, but *when*.

We learned from epidemiological linkage of the initial human SARS cases to wild animals that SARS is zoonotic in origin. This finding led to strict bans in the wild meat trade and contact bans between people and animal disease reservoirs.

It also was learned that sharing epidemiological and clinical data among affected countries was pivotal in identifying the SARS virus and in enforcing coordinated efforts to control the spread of the disease. These control procedures included: compulsory isolation of cases, surveillance of contacts, and the temporary closing of schools in affected areas. These all are inexpensive, low-tech methods that have been used successfully for decades; it was the coordination of these methods among affected countries, however, that made these efforts successful.

Managing and controlling emerging diseases such as SARS depends on rapidly identifying the mode of transmission and quickly implementing a control strategy. SARS is spread by person-to-person contact, both by direct and indirect contact with the infectious respiratory droplets. Nosocomial transmission of SARS was facilitated by the use of nebulizers, intubation, and cardiopulmonary resuscitation (CPR). As a result, health care personnel, including nurses and doctors, were infected and even died. Strategies to limit spreading infectious disease outbreaks include:

- isolation and quarantine of patients and potentially affected cases; hospitals must have special wards for isolating infectious cases;

- strictly following hand washing protocols;

- using protective equipment—hospital personnel and patients' families should use masks, gloves, and eye protection around patients; and

- limiting SARS patients' exposure to procedures that could spread the disease, such as intubation and nebulization.

Given the mobility of the human population and therefore the real risk of a global epidemic, collaboration of international authorities such as the World Health Organization and other governmental agencies such as the Centers for Disease Control and Prevention is very important to verify outbreaks, investigate their severity, and to evaluate control measures.

Many lessons were learned from the first exposure to SARS. In March 2008, the Hong Kong government ordered all kindergarten and primary schools to be closed for two weeks during an outbreak of influenza. Health Secretary York Chow said that Yuen Kwok-Yung, who had helped study Hong Kong's outbreak of SARS four years earlier would head a panel of scientists studying the deaths of three children over that previous week.

Based on lessons from SARS, private industry is taking measures to ensure that employees keep healthy and do not contribute to the spread of the disease. Many made contingency plans during this influenza outbreak. Consider the following memo from Deutsche Bank:

> Deutsche Bank being a global bank, our relationship managers are on the road all the time and when countries put up travel restrictions or quarantine measures, that impacted the ways that business was conducted. There were also a lot of other operational difficulties faced by organizations. For example, in some locations or some organizations, they would implement a quarantine period for anyone coming from Asia. You had to quarantine yourself for between 5 to 15 days before you were allowed to come into the office. And that created a lot of disruption to the work.[2]

As a precautionary measure, the bank sent its entire team of bond traders home to be quarantined for ten days.

We are in that quiet time before the storm of the next major disease outbreak, but unfortunately, we don't know whether that quiet time will last for six months, a year, four years, or a decade.

Now, however, we know better than to pat ourselves on the back. SARS will come back again. If only one monkey in the Brazilian rain forest is infected with the virus or even if it continues in an isolated village in a remote South Pacific atoll, it will find its way back to more heavily populated areas again. The next outbreak of the SARS virus may follow the same pattern as the 2003 outbreak, or it may be an entirely new strain of the virus that has different characteristics.

What might trigger the next outbreak is unknown. It can come from the importation of a pet from abroad, or from American tourists exploring a jungle somewhere in Asia, from exposure by health workers at a mission health center, or from any one of a number of scenarios. Viruses that are responsible for reemerging diseases have a great ability to mutate, evolve, and adapt to new hosts.

What we do know is that we should be able to deal with reemergence more rapidly and efficiently than ever before. Today we can use PCR methods to identify the virus more quickly and use the Internet to communicate warnings and cautions to stop the virus from spreading before many people have been exposed.

While the science and technology have improved, there are still no guarantees that we are better off than in 2003 when the first round of SARS was prevalent. We cannot be certain that some countries will acknowledge the presence of the virus locally since that means the temporary end of tourist and business visits, and in some quarters it signifies an insufficient level of public health and hygiene or a blemish on that nation's reputation.

RETROSPECTIVE EXAMINATION OF SARS

The WHO issued its first-ever travel advisory during the 2003 SARS outbreak. WHO recommended the postponement of all but essential travel to Hong Kong and to China's Guangdong Province, and later the organization added similar advisories against travel to Toronto and Beijing. WHO also issued a global health alert as SARS was quickly spreading from Hong Kong to Vietnam and Toronto. The alert was meant to contain the disease and to protect countries that did not have the infrastructure to deal with SARS risks. The world community was afraid and ill-prepared to face a world epidemic, which is why WHO and individual governments acted firmly to control the SARS spread that could have had even more disastrous consequences.

That travel advisory and the threat of SARS had unparalleled negative economic consequences in the travel industry, and it was a reminder that an outbreak of a highly contagious disease can put the whole world at risk of an epidemic regardless of where it starts.

During the SARS outbreak, regional governments in Canada, Vietnam, and Hong Kong collected clinical and epidemiological data to unlock clues about the disease while also having the simultaneous challenge of managing and controlling the outbreak. The WHO offered these countries epidemiological, laboratory, and clinical support in addition to coordinating an international multicenter effort in ten countries to identify the causative agent and to develop a diagnostic test. WHO also issued, early on, a case definition for the identification of SARS cases.

- A suspect case was anyone with fever and respiratory symptoms.

- A probable case was someone who had had close contact with a person diagnosed with SARS and/or who had a history of travel to a SARS-infected area.

- A suspect case had all of the above and an X-ray confirming pneumonia.

Subsequently the definition of a SARS case was refined. It consisted of all of the above criteria plus the absence of an alternative diagnosis.

The SARS outbreak was ultimately controlled by isolating cases, tracing and quarantining contacts, and maintaining vigilance in surveillance efforts.

FUTURE RESPONSES TO SARS

It is probably wishful thinking that we have seen the last of SARS. It requires that only a few animals harboring the virus come into close contact with humans, to bring about the reality of a potentially global epidemic. There are two lines of defense before a virus becomes a problem. The first, preventing the introduction of diseases or its reemergence, is essentially impossible. The second, containing or preventing a **zoonosis**, is a critical imperative.

It appears that the 2003 cases of SARS resulted from interspecies transmission from wild game markets to humans. Health authorities were initially unprepared for the SARS outbreak, and lack of epidemiological knowledge, such as modes of transmission and source of the disease, made it impossible to activate effective countermeasures right away. We learned that forthright, honest, immediate acknowledgement of the disease can limit its spread and get international health agencies and experts involved rapidly.

We learned that some new technologies, such as PCR tests, can make immediate and significant contributions to epidemiologic investigations. Now we should be able to identify the responsible virus and know whether it should be a source of worry or not. Using monoclonal techniques, it becomes possible to prepare large quantities of vaccine rapidly. We learned that some very old, tried-and-true disease-fighting measures, such as quarantine, are still important and effective in the twenty-first century.

We learned that while nations do not like to acknowledge serious diseases of possible epidemic proportions, it is essential that public health agencies notify the WHO and neighboring country's health agencies of potential epidemics and work in coordination. Such responsiveness provides the proper means to fight the epidemic.

In January 2004 there was a meeting of the Royal Society in London to consider the lessons learned from the SARS outbreak. The meeting credited the laboratories that coordinated and cooperated in 17 different countries, patient isolation, travel restrictions, and contact precautions as the efforts that successfully limited further transmission of the disease. Also credited was a new tool—mathematical models—for providing a framework for evaluation of alternative control measures, and prediction about the future course of the epidemic.

Moreover, the clear success of the WHO in catalyzing global collaboration in containing SARS sufficiently moved the World Health Assembly to grant WHO greater authority to verify future outbreaks, conduct investigations of outbreak severity, and to evaluate the adequacy of control measures.

The SARS epidemic of 2003 was a wake-up call regarding the risks of global epidemics. Had there been just a little more delay, we could have had a serious international catastrophe with millions sick or dead; international business could have been brought to a standstill.

Lastly, ever since the 2003 SARS outbreak, health authorities understand that time is a weapon in their hands, and they cannot waste time to implement preventive measures when an alert of a virus threat exists.

Sometimes, however, these lessons are forgotten. On May 7, 2008, *The Wall Street Journal* reported: "China's tight-lipped response to a dangerous outbreak of a common childhood illness suggests that its propaganda machine, geared to control political discourse, still operates erratically when it comes to public health."[3] It appears that an outbreak of hand, foot, and mouth disease has already killed more than 20 children.

Everything presented in this chapter, and indeed, in this book, testifies to the limited power and control we humans have in combating acts of nature. Just like hurricanes or tornadoes, snowstorms or droughts, we have very limited tools to modify or change the course of nature.

Again and again, our best strategy is prevention. Specifically regarding SARS, if we continue to be vigilant in culling ill animals and employing quarantine, isolation, and open communication when infections are discovered, we will be able to at least contain the disease and minimize its impact, if not eliminate it.

Appendix

A Timeline of the SARS Outbreak

November 16, 2002 The first case of atypical pneumonia is reported in Guangdong Province, located in southern China.

February 26, 2003 The first cases of unusual pneumonia are reported in Hanoi, Vietnam.

February 28, 2003 Dr. Carlo Urbani of the World Health Organization (WHO) examines a Chinese-American businessman at a French hospital in Hanoi, Vietnam.

March 10, 2003 Urbani reports an unusual outbreak of the illness, which he names "sudden acute respiratory syndrome," or "SARS," to the main office of the WHO. He states that 22 health care workers at the hospital have been infected.

March 11, 2003 Health care workers in Hong Kong fall ill in a similar outbreak of mysterious respiratory disease; Urbani falls ill.

March 12, 2003 The WHO puts out a global alert, warning the public about the new infectious disease that has been found in both Vietnam and Hong Kong.

March 15, 2003 The WHO issues a global health alert about the disease, and issues a case definition of SARS. Cases in Singapore and Canada are also identified. The alert includes a rare travel advisory for international travelers, medical professionals, and health authorities.

March 17, 2003 An international network of 11 leading research laboratories begin work to determine the cause of SARS.

March 24, 2003 Centers for Disease Control and Prevention (CDC) officials offer the first evidence that a new strain of a coronavirus might be the cause of SARS.

March 29, 2003 Urbani, who identified the first case of SARS, dies from the disease.

April 2, 2003 The WHO issues a travel warning, advising that any nonessential travel to Hong Kong and the Guangdong area of China be postponed.

April 3, 2003 A WHO-sponsored team of infectious disease experts goes to Guangdong to learn more about the outbreak.

April 4, 2003 U.S. President George W. Bush adds SARS to the list of diseases that require suspected patients to be quarantined. This gives the CDC the power to isolate people who might have been exposed to the disease.

April 9, 2003	The WHO investigative team in Guangdong gives its first report. The team says it has found evidence of "super-spreaders" who can infect as many as 100 people each.
April 12, 2003	Canadian health researchers announce that they have completed the first successful sequencing of the genome of the coronavirus believed to cause SARS.
April 14, 2003	CDC officials announce that they have sequenced a nearly identical strain of the SARS-related coronavirus.
April 16, 2003	A new form of a coronavirus never before seen in humans is confirmed as the cause of SARS, after being put to the test using Koch's postulates.
April 22, 2003	The CDC issues a health alert for travelers to Toronto, which is the center of the Canadian SARS outbreak.
April 23, 2003	The WHO adds Toronto, Beijing, and the Shanxi Province of China to the list of places international travelers should avoid to reduce the risk of contracting SARS. WHO officials say the travel advisory will remain in effect for at least the next three weeks.
April 28, 2003	The WHO removes Vietnam from list of SARS-affected areas, after Vietnam successfully contains its SARS outbreak. The WHO also lifts the travel advisory to Hanoi, Vietnam.
April 29, 2003	The WHO lifts its warning against nonessential travel to Toronto, Canada, after the area has reported no new cases for 20 days.
May 6, 2003	The CDC lifts its travel advisory for Singapore because no new cases of SARS had been reported there for 20 days.
May 15, 2003	The CDC removes its travel alert for Hanoi, Vietnam, after 30 days have passed since the last report of SARS there.
May 17, 2003	The WHO extends its travel warning to include Hebei Province, China. A similar warning to cancel or postpone all nonessential travel is in effect for Hong Kong, Taipei, Taiwan, and several other areas of mainland China, including Beijing, Guangdong, Inner Mongolia, Shanxi, and Tianjin.

May 20, 2003	The CDC lifts its travel warning for Toronto, Canada.
May 23, 2003	The WHO lifts its advisory against nonessential travel to Hong Kong and the Guangdong province of China.
May 26, 2003	The WHO lists Toronto, Canada, as an area where SARS has recently been transmitted locally after Canadian health officials report new clusters of 26 suspect and eight probable SARS cases.
May 31, 2003	The WHO takes Singapore off its list of areas where SARS has been transmitted locally.
June 13, 2003	The WHO lifts its travel restriction on nonessential travel to several provinces in China, including Hebei, Inner Mongolia, Shanxi, and Tianjin.
June 17, 2003	The WHO lifts its travel warning against nonessential travel to Taiwan. The CDC makes its travel warning for mainland China a less-severe alert, although a travel warning from both the CDC and the WHO remains in effect for Beijing.
June 23, 2003	The WHO removes Hong Kong from its list of areas with recent local SARS transmission.
June 24, 2003	The WHO removes its last remaining SARS travel warning for Beijing, China.
June 25, 2003	The CDC downgrades its SARS travel advice for Beijing, China, and Taiwan from "advisory" to "alert" status, which simply informs travelers of a SARS health concern and advises them to take precautions.
July 2, 2003	The WHO removes Toronto, Canada, from its list of areas with recent local SARS transmission.
July 8, 2003	The CDC lifts its SARS travel alert for Toronto, Canada.
July 9, 2003	The CDC lifts its SARS travel alert for Hong Kong retroactively to July 1 because the last SARS case there was reported on May 31.
August 2003	The WHO declares the SARS epidemic over.
January 2004	Royal Society in London meets to consider SARS lessons learned.
2005–2009	Work on vaccine in progress.

Notes

Chapter 1

1. Secretariat's report to the World Health Organization's Executive Board, January 2004.

Chapter 2

1. S. K. P. Lau, P. C. Y. Woo, K. S. M. Li, Y. Huang, H.-W. Tsoi, B. H. L. Wong, S. S. Y. Wong, S.-Y. Leung, K.-H. Chan, and K.-Y. Yuen, "Severe Acute Respiratory Syndrome Coronavirus-Like Virus in Chinese Horseshoe Bats," *Proceedings National Academy of Sciences USA*, 102, 39 (2005): 14040–14045.

2. Daniel Janies, "Evolutionary History of SARS Supports Bats as Virus Source," http://www.eurekalert.org/pub_releases/2008-02/osu-eho021908.php (accessed January 27, 2009).

Chapter 5

1. J. E. Martin, M. K. Louder, L. A. Holman, I. J. Gordon, et. al., "A SARS DNA Vaccine Induces Neutralizing Antibody and Cellular Immune Responses in Healthy Adults in a Phase I Clinical Trial," *Vaccine*, 26, 50 (November 25, 2008): 6338–6343.

Chapter 8

1. R. W. Pinner, S. M. Tench, L. Simmonsen, et. al., "1996 Trends in Infectious Diseases Mortality in the United States," *Journal of the American Medical Association* 275 (1996): 189–193.

2. Kenny Seow, "Deutsche Bank Singapore Financial Sector Lessons Learned from SARS," University of Pittsburgh Medical Center, http://www.upmc-biosecurity. org/website/events/2005_bullsbears-birds/speakers/seow/transcript.html (accessed April 15, 2009).

3. N. Zamiska, "China's Delay in Reporting Outbreak Creates a Stir," *The Wall Street Journal*, (May 7, 2008). http://online.wsj.com/article/SB120999586546267507.html (accessed April 15, 2009).

Glossary

ACE2—Angiotensin converting enzyme 2, a protein known for its role in regulating blood pressure. It has been identified as a SARS-CoV functional receptor.

airborne transmission—Spread by or through the air.

antibacterial—Having the properties of an antibiotic; able to kill bacteria or suppress their growth and reproduction.

antibiotic—A substance that destroys bacteria or suppresses their growth or reproduction.

antibody—Blood protein that is produced in response to the presence of a foreign substance (such as a bacterium or virus) in the body.

antiviral—Drugs that stimulate cellular defenses against viruses, reducing cell DNA synthesis and making cells more resistant to viral genes.

asymptomatic—Showing no symptoms of a disease.

atypical pneumonia—Pneumonia (a respiratory infection) that does not respond to penicillin, but does respond to such antibiotics as tetracycline and erythromycin.

bronchoscopy—A medical procedure that allows the doctor to view the bronchi (small air sacs) of the lungs.

capsid—Protein coat that surrounds a virus.

case fatality rate—The proportion or percentage of people with a disease who die from it, e.g., if 100 people get a disease and 2 die, the case fatality rate is 2 percent.

cilia—The fine hairlike projections from certain types of cells. Cilia line the respiratory tract.

cluster—A group of cases of a disease, closely linked in time and place.

communicable disease—A disease that is easily transmitted between people.

coronavirus (CoV)—Group of viruses that have a crown-like appearance and are responsible for most respiratory infections.

CoV—Coronavirus.

cytokines—Protein molecules secreted by cells of the immune system, which serve to replicate the immune system.

cytoplasm—General term that applies to all the material found in the interior of a living cell, excluding the nucleus.

DNA (deoxyribonucleic acid)—The genetic material of nearly all living organisms, which controls heredity and is located in the cell nucleus.

emerging infectious disease—An infectious disease whose incidence has increased in the past 20 years and threatens to increase in the near future.

endotracheal intubation—A procedure where a tube is placed down the windpipe (trachea) to allow the patient to breathe with the help of a mechanical ventilator.

epidemic—A rapid increase in the numbers of cases of an infection.

epidemiology—Study of the incidence, distribution, and control of diseases or patterns in populations.

epithelial—Relating to the epithelium, which are the tissues that line the body's cavities.

epitope—The site on the surface of an antigen molecule to which an antibody attatches.

febrile—Having a fever.

fibrogranulative tissue—The tissues of the airways.

genome—An organism's genetic material.

genomic—Pertaining to the genome; all of the genetic information possessed by an organism.

germ theory—A theory which states that diseases are caused by microorganisms.

HCoV (human coronavirus)—A new coronavirus responsible for causing severe acute respiratory syndrome (SARS) in humans.

host—A person or other living organism that can be infected by an infectious agent under natural conditions.

immunomodulatory—Capable of modifying or regulating one or more immune functions.

incidence—The rate at which new cases of infection arise in a population.

incubation period—The time that elapses between infection and the appearance of symptoms of a disease.

index case—First patient to come down with a particular disease during an outbreak.

infectious—Able to be transmitted from one person to another.

inflammatory—A response of body tissue to injury or irritation; complex biological response of vascular tissues to harmful stimuli such as pathogens, damaged cells, and irritants.

innate immune system—The immunity an organism is born with. The adaptive immune system is the immunity an organism develops in response to various microorganisms in its environment.

inoculum—A substance or organism that is introduced into surroundings suited to cell growth.

interferon—A naturally occurring substance that interferes with the ability of viruses to reproduce. It also boosts the immune system.

isolation—The separation of persons who have a specific infectious illness from those who are healthy.

leukopenia—An abnormal lowering of the blood white cell count.

lymphopenia—Reduction in the number of lymphocytes (one kind of white blood cell).

macrophage—A large phagocyte or immune system cells that devours invading pathogens.

microorganism—An organism of a very small (microscopic) size.

mortality—The per capita death rate in a population.

nebulizer—A device used to deliver medicine directly to the lungs via an inhalable spray.

necrosis—The localized death of living cells and tissues.

nosocomial—Acquired in a hospital.

nucleocapsid—The genome (DNA or RNA) of a virus and the protein coat surrounding the capsid.

oral-fecal transmission—The spread of the disease through the contamination of food with feces. This may occur when someone who has a disease does not wash his or her hands properly after using the bathroom, then prepares or otherwise touches food or utensils that another person puts into his or her mouth.

ORF—Open reading frames, a portion of an organism's genome, which contains a sequence of bases that could potentially encode a protein.

outbreak—A sudden increase in the number of cases of a disease in a particular area; an epidemic.

pathogen—Any disease-producing microorganism.

pathogenesis—The step-by-step development of a disease.

peplomers—Subunits of a virus particle.

polymerase chain reaction (PCR)—A technique widely used in molecular biology to amplify a piece of DNA.

prevalence—The proportion of the host population infected at a given time.

prophylactic—Preventative measure.

proteases—Enzymes that digest proteins.

quarantine—The enforced isolation or restriction of free movement of a patient to avoid the spread of a contagious disease.

replicase—An enzyme that catalyzes the replication of RNA from an RNA template.

replicate—When DNA makes copies of itself as a cell divides.

RNA (ribonucleic acid)—Substance involved in the transmission of genetic information.

RT-PCR (reverse transcription–polymerase chain reaction)—A method for finding and determing the kind of mRNA (messenger RNA; a copy of genetic information from an organism's DNA) in a sample of cells from an organism.

sensitivity—Repsponsivity to external stimuli; susceptibility to a pathogen.

sputum induction—A process to remove sputum (mucus and other fluid) from the lungs.

squamous metaplasia—Benign (noncancerous) changes in the epithelial linings of certain organs within the body.

subpleural proliferation—The growth of tissues in the lungs in response to damage done by disease or injury.

thrombocytopenia—An abnormally low number of thrombocytes (platelets).

vaccine—Substance that triggers the production of antibodies that protect against pathogens.

viral load—The amount of virus that is present in an infected person's bloodstream.

virion—A complete virus particle with its DNA or RNA core and protein coat as it exits the host cell. Also called a viral particle.

virulent—Easily able to overwhelm body immune defenses and cause disease.

virus—A tiny microorganism that is capable of replication, but only when it is inside living cells.

zoonosis—An infectious disease that can be transmitted by a vector from other animals, both wild and domestic, to humans.

Anand, Kanchan, John Ziebuhr, Parvesh Wadhwani, et al. "Coronavirus Main Proteinase Structure: Basis for Design of Anti-SARS Drugs." *Science* 300 (2003): 1763–1767.

The Bantam Medical Dictionary, 2d ed. New York: Market House Books Ltd., 1996.

Bartlam Mark, Haitao Yang and Zihe Rao. "Structural Insights into SARS Coronavirus Proteins." *Current Opinion in Structural Biology* 15 (2005): 664-672.

Bastur, S. V., et al. "SARS: A Local Public Health Perspective." *Canadian Journal of Public Health* 95, no. 1 (2004): 22–24.

Berkow, Robert, ed. "Viral Infections." *The Merck Manual of Medical Information Home Edition.* Whitehouse, N.J.: Merck and Co., 1997.

Cameron, Peter A, Michael Schull, and Matthew Cooke. "The Impending Influenza Pandemic: Lessons from SARS for Hospital Practice." *MJA* 185, 4 (2006):189–190.

Centers for Disease Control and Prevention. "About CDC." Available online. URL: http://www.cdc.gov/aboutcdc.htm. Updated February 6, 2009.

———. "Clinical Guidance on the Identification and Evaluation of Possible SARS-CoV Disease among Persons Presenting with Community-Acquired Illness Version 2." (January 8, 2004). Available online. URL: http://www.cdc. gov/ncidod/sars/clinicalguidance.htm.

———. "Division of Global Migration and Quarantine. History of Quarantine." Available online. URL: http://www.cdc.gov/ncidod/dq/ history.htm. Accessed April 15, 2009.

———. "Evaluation and Management of Patients Requiring Hospitalization." May 3, 2005. Available online. Accessed April 15, 2009. URL: http://www.cdc. gov/ncidod/sars/clinical-guidance 1.htm.

———. "History of CDC." *Morbidity and Mortality Weekly Report* 45 (1996): 526–528.

———. "In the Absence of SARS-CoV Transmission Worldwide: Guidance for Surveillance, Clinical and Laboratory Evaluation, and Reporting Version 2." January 21, 2004. Available online. URL: http://www.cdc.gov/ ncidod/sars/absenceofsars.htm.

———. "Preliminary Clinical Description of Severe Acute Respiratory Syndrome." *Morbidity and Mortality Weekly Report* 52 (2003): 255–256. Available online. URL: http://www.cdc.gov/mmwr/preview/mmwrhtml/.

———. "Public Health Guidance for Community-Level Preparedness and Response to Severe Acute Respiratory Syndrome (SARS) Version 2.

Community-Based Control Measures." January 8, 2004. Available online. URL: http://www.cdc.gov/ncidod/sars/guidance/D/community.htm.

————. "Public Health Guidance for Community-Level Preparedness and Response to Severe Acute Respiratory Syndrome (SARS) Version 2. Management of SARS Patients in Isolation." May 3, 2005. Available online. URL: http://www.cdc.gov/ncidod/sars/guidance/D/isolation.htm.

————. "Public Health Guidance for Community-Level Preparedness and Response to Severe Acute Respiratory Syndrome (SARS) Version 2. Rationale and Goals. Center for Disease Control and Prevention." January 8, 2004. Available online. URL: http://www.cd.c.gov/ncidod/sars/guidance/D/rationale.htm.

————. "Public Health Guidance for Community-Level Preparedness and Response to Severe Acute Respiratory Syndrome (SARS) Version 2. Summary." January 8, 2003. Available online. URL: http://www.cdc.gov/ncidod/sars/guidance/D/summary.htm.

————. "Severe Acute Respiratory Syndrome." *Morbidity and Mortality Weekly Report* 2003–2004. May 3, 2005. Available online. URL: http://www.cdc.gov/mmwr/mguide_sars.html.

————. "Severe Acute Respiratory Syndrome: Basic Information About SARS." January 13, 2004. Available online. URL: http://www.cdc.gov/ncidod/sars/factsheet.htm.

————. "Severe Acute Respiratory Syndrome (SARS): Fact Sheet on Isolation and Quarantine." January 20, 2004. Available online. URL: http://www.cdc.gov/ncidod/sars/isolationquaratine.htm.

————. "Threshold Determinants for the Use of Community Containment Measures." May 3, 2005. Available online. URL: http://www.cdc.gov/ncidod/sars/guidance/D/app4.htm.

Chan, P., et al. "Severe Acute Respiratory Syndrome-Associated Coronavirus Infection." *Emerging Infectious Diseases* 9 (11) (2003): 1453–1454.

Cheng ,V. C., S. K. Lau, P. C. Woo, and K. Y. Yuen. "Severe Acute Respiratory Syndrome Coronavirus as an Agent of Emerging and Re-emerging Infection." *Clinical Microbiology Review* 20, 4 (October 2007): 660–694.

Cohen, Jon. "Do Clinical Masks Stop SARS?" *Slate,* April 2003. Available online. URL: http://slate.msn.com.

Dye, Chris, and Nigel Gay. "Modeling the SARS Epidemic." *Science* 300 (2003): 1884–1885.

Feng, Youjun, and George F. Gao. "Towards Our Understanding of SARS-CoV, and Emerging and Devastating but Quickly Conquered Virus." *Comp. Immun. Microbiol.Infect. Dis.* 30 (2007): 309–327.

Gu, Jiang and Christine Korteweg. "Pathology and Pathogenesis of Severe Acute Respiratory Syndrome." *Am. J. Pathol.* 170, 4 (April 2007): 1136–1147.

Guan, Y., B. J. Zheng, Y. Q. He, et al. "Isolation and Characterization of Viruses Related to the SARS Coronavirus from Animals in Southern China." *Science* 302 (2003): 276–278.

Holmes, Kathryn, and Luis Enjuanes. "The SARS Coronavirus: A Postgenomic Era." *Science* 300 (2003): 1377–1378.

Hsu, Ly, C. C. Lee, J. A. Green, et al. "Severe Acute Respiratory Syndrome (SARS) in Singapore: Clinical Features of Index Patients and Initial Contacts." *Emerging Infectious Diseases* 9 (2003): 713–717. Available online. URL: http://www.cdc.gov/ncidod/EID/vol0no6.

Hung, Lee Shiu. "The SARS Epidemic in Hong Kong: What Lessons Have We Learned?" *Journal of the Royal Society of Medicine* Vol. 96, 8 (August 2003): 374–378.

International Herald Tribune. Briefly International. "Hong Kong Kindergartens to Close Because of Flu Outbreak." *International Herald Tribune.* Thursday, March 13, 2008.

Jiang, Shibo, Yuxian He, and Shuwen Liu. "SARS Vaccine Development." *Emerging Infectious Diseases* 11, 7 (July 2005): 1016–1020.

Kamps, Bernd Sebastian, and Khristian Hoffmann, eds. *SARS Reference*, 3rd ed. Flying Publisher, 2003, pp. 1–172. Available online. URL: http://www.SARSreference.com.

Kuhn, Jens H., Wenhui Li, Sheli R. Rodoshitzky, Hyeryun Choe, and Michael Farzan. "Severe Acute Respiratory Syndrome Coronavirus Entry as a Target of Antiviral Therapies." *Antiviral Activity* 12, 4 (2007): 639–650.

Lipsitch, Mar, Ted Cohen, Ben Cooper, et al. "Transmission Dynamics and Control of Severe Acute Respiratory Syndrome." *Science* 300 (2003): 1966–1970.

Li, Wenhui, Michel J. Moore, Natalya Vasilieva, Jianhua Sui, et al. "Angiotensin-Converting Enzyme 2 Is a Functional Receptor for the SARS Coronavirus." *Nature* 426, 27 (November 2003).

Liu, X., M. Zhang, L. He, P. Li, and Y. Kang. "Chinese Herbs Combined with Western Medicines for Severe Acute Respiratory (SARS) Syndrome." *Cochrane Database of Systematic Review,* 1, Article number CD004882.DOI (2006).

Lyons, A., and J. Petrucelli. *Medicine: An Illustrated History.* New York: Harry N. Abrams, Inc., 1987.

Maglen, Krista. "The First Line of Defense: British Quarantine and the Port Sanitary Authority in the Nineteenth Century." *Social History of Medicine* 15 (2000): 413–428.

Marra, Marco, Steve Jones, Caroline Astell, et al. "The Genome Sequence of the SARS-Associated Coronavirus." *Science* 300 (2003): 1399–1404.

Maybury, Bonnie A., and Pamela M. Peters. "Vaccines: How and Why?" Available online. URL: http://www.accessexcellence.org/AE/AEC/CC/vaccines_how_why.html. Accessed April 15, 2009.

Merson, Michael. "SARS Proved Health Is Global Public Good." *YaleGlobal* 24 (September 2003). Available online. URL: http://yaleglobal.yale.edu/display.article?id=2503.

Ministry of Health and Long Term Care, Ontario. "SARS. Directive: Discharge of SARS Patients." Directive DS03-04. December 4, 2003.

Olsen, S., et al. "Transmission of the Severe Acute Respiratory Syndrome in Aircraft." *New England Journal of Medicine* 349 (25) (2003): 2426–2422.

Pang, X., et al. "Evaluation of Control Measures Implemented in the Severe Acute Respiratory Syndrome Outbreak in Beijing." *Journal of the American Medical Association* 290, 24 (2003): 3215–3221.

Peiris, J. S., C. M. Chu, V. C. Cheng, et al. "Clinical Progression and Viral Load in a Community Outbreak of Coronavirus-Associated SARS Pneumonia: A Prospective Study." *Lancet* 361 (2003): 1767–1772. Available online. URL: http://image.thelancet.com/extras/03art347.

Poon, L. L. M., Y. Guan, J. M. Nicholss, K. Y. Yuen, and J. S. Peiris. "The Etiology, Origins, and Diagnosis of Severe Acute Respiratory Syndrome." *The Lancet Infectious Diseases* 4 (November 2004).

Pottinger, Matt. "Megadoses of Steroids Devastated Many Chinese SARS Patients." *Wall Street Journal*, December 23, 2003. Available online. URL: http://www.sarswatch.org/comments.php.

Ruan, Y. J., C. L. Wei, et al. "Comparative Full-Length Genome Sequence Analysis of 14 SARS Coronavirus Isolates and Common Mutations Associates with Putative Origins of Infection." *Lancet* 361 (2003): 1779–1785. Available online. URL: http://image.thelancet.com/extras/03art445.

Sampathkumar, Priya, Zelalem Temesgen, Thomas Smith, et al. "SARS: Epidemiology, Clinical Presentation, Management, and Infection Control Measures." *Mayo Clinic Proceedings* 78 (2003): 882–890.

"SARS." *Mayo Clinic Proceedings* 78 (2003): 883.

Satija, Namita, and Sunil K. Lal. "The Molecular Biology of SARS Coronavirus." *Ann. N.Y. Acad. Sci.* 1102 (2007): 26–38.

Stockman, Lauren J., Richard Bellamy, Paul Garner. "SARS: Systematic Review of Treatment Effects." *PLOS* 3, 9 (September 2006): 1525–1531.

Tsunetsuyu-Yokota, Yasuko, Kazuo Ohnishi, and Toshitada Takemori. "Severe Acute Respiratory Syndrome (SARS) Coronavirus: Application of Monoclonal Antibodies and Development of an Effective Vaccine." *Medical Virology* 16, 2 (March–April 2006): 117–131.

Veuzner, Gerhard. *500 Years of Medicine.* New York: Tapliger Publishing Co., 1972.

Wang, Chen G. "Research Work on SARS Has to be Strengthened in China." *Chinese Medical Journal* 116 (7) (2003): 963–964.

Wilder-Smith, Annelies. "The Severe Acute Respiratory Syndrome: Impact on Travel and Tourism." *Travel Medicine and Infectious Disease* 4 (2006): 53–60.

Wong, Janet. "SARS Outbreak Has University Impact." March 31, 2003. Available online. URL: http://www.news.utoronto.ca/bin4/030331c.asp.

World Health Organization. "Cumulative Number of Reported Probable Cases of Severe Respiratory Syndrome (SARS)." November 1, 2002–May 8, 2003. Available online. URL: http://www.who.int/csr/sarscountry/.

———. "Global Search for SARS Vaccine Gains Momentum." November, 2, 2003. Available online. URL: http://www.who.int/mediacentre/releases/2003/pr83/en/.

———. "SARS Epidemiology to Date." April, 11, 2003. Available online. URL: http://www.who.int/csr/sars/epi2003_04_11/en/.

———. "Use of Laboratory Methods for SARS Diagnosis." Available online. URL: http://www.who.int/csr/sars/labmethods/en/.

Wyngaarden, James B., and Lloyd H. Smith. "Viral Diseases." *Textbook of Medicine*, 15th ed. Philadelphia: W. B. Saunders Co., 1982.

Xin, Xiao. "First SARS Vaccine Tested." Available online. URL: http://www.china daily.com.cn/english/doc/200405/25/content_333679.htm.

Yeun, Kap-Sun, and Nicholas Meanwell. "Recent Developments in the Virology and Antiviral Research of Severe Acute Respiratory Coronavirus." *Infectious Disorders-Drug Targets* 20207, 7: 29–41.

Zamiska, Nicholas. "China's Delay in Reporting Outbreak Creates a Stir." *The Wall Street Journal.* May 7, 2008.

Zhi, Yan, James Wilson, and Hao Shen. "SARS Vaccine: Progress and Challenge." *Cellular & Molecular Immunology* Vol 2, 2 (April 2005):101-105.

Further Resources

Books

Abraham, Thomas. *Twenty-first Century Plague: The Story of SARS*. Baltimore: Johns Hopkins University Press, 2005.

Brookes, Timothy J. *Behind the Mask: How the World Survived SARS, the First Epidemic of the Twenty-first Century*. Washington, D.C.: American Public Health Association, 2005.

Chung Leung, Ping, and Eng Eong Ooi, eds. *SARS War: Combating the Disease in Singapore*. River Edge, NJ: World Scientific, 2003.

Goudsmit, Jaap. *Viral Fitness: The Next SARS and West Nile in the Making*. New York: Oxford University Press, 2004.

Kasper, Dennis L., Eugene Braunwald, Anthony Fauci, Stephen L. Hauser, and Dan L. Longo, eds. *Harrison's Principles of Internal Medicine*, 16th ed. New York: McGraw-Hill, 2004.

Loh, Christine. *At the Epicentre: Hong Kong and the SARS Outbreak*. Aberdeen, Hong Kong: Hong Kong University Press, 2004.

Web Sites

The Centers for Disease Control and Prevention
http://www.cdc.gov

Health Canada
http://www.hc-sc.gc.ca

Medline Plus
http://medlineplus.gov

The National Institutes of Health
http://www.nih.gov

SARS Reference
http://www.sarsreference.com

The World Health Organization
http://www.who.int

Index

ACE2. *See* angiotensin converting enzyme 2

acquired immunodeficiency syndrome (AIDS) , 6, 7, 87

acute diarrhea, 6

AIDS. *See* acquired immunodeficiency syndrome

airborne transmission, 39. *See also* SARS, transmission of

alert. *See* health alert

angiotensin converting enzyme 2 (ACE2), 37–38

antibiotics, 64–65, 66

antibodies, 30, 50

anti-infective drugs, 7. *See also* drugs

antiviral drugs, 66. *See also* drugs

Aspergillus, 41

asymptomatic, 21

Atlanta, Georgia, 47, 76

atypical pneumonia, 17, 33

avian flu, 13, 87

avian influenza A (H5N1), 6

avian influenza virus, 89

B cells, 30

Bangkok, 10

Bangkok Hospital, 11

bats, 36

bed nets, 7

Beijing, China, 14, 79, 93

bird flu. *See* avian flu

blood cells, white, 20

Bovine Spongiform Encephalopathy (BSE), 6

Brazzaville, Republic of Congo, 18

bronchoalveolar lavage, 34

bronchoscopy, 39

BSE. *See* Bovine Spongiform Encephalopathy

Bureau of Citizenship and Immigration Services, 47

Cairo, Egypt, 19

Canada
  case cluster, 34
  control and management of SARS, 94
  SARS cluster in hospital, 19
  SARS transmission, 12, 18, 45, 89
  tourism, impact of SARS on, 13
  travel advisory, 49, 93

Canadian Health Authorities, 51

capsid, 27

cardiopulmonary resuscitation (CPR), 91

case fatality rate, 20

CDC. *See* Centers for Disease Control and Prevention

Centers for Disease Control and Prevention (CDC), 10
  control and management of SARS, 83, 91
  described, 76
  diagnosis guidelines, 58
  disease outbreak information, 81, 91
  Division of Global Migration and Quarantine, 47
  National Center for Preparedness, Detection, and Control of Infectious Diseases, 47
  prevention recommendations, 51, 54, 75

Chamberland (Pasteur's assistant), 25

Cheng, Johnny, 8–9, 10–11, 17

Chicago, Illinois, 47

China, 97
  economic effects of SARS, 79, 82
  first case of human SARS, 89
  herbal medicines, 67
  political barriers, 90
  SARS origins and spread, 15–20, 36
  SARS research , 35–36
  SARS transmission, 12, 14
  travel advisory, 49, 93
  travel restrictions, 81
  vaccines, 71

Chinese ferret badger, 54

Chinese herbal remedies. *See* herbal remedies

Chow, York, 92

cilia, 29, 41

civet, 32, 35–36, 54

clusters, 17

communicable disease, 6, 10

complex virus, 31

condoms, 7

Copenhagen, Denmark, 19

coronavirus (CoV), 13

corticosteroids, 67

CoV. *See* coronavirus

CPR. *See* cardiopulmonary resuscitation

Customs and Border Protection, 47
cytokines, 67–68

deoxyribonucleic acid. *See* DNA
Department of Health and Human
    Services, 76
Deutsche Bank, 92
diagnosis of SARS. *See* SARS, diagnosis of
diarrheal disease, 87
DNA (deoxyribonucleic acid), 27, 28
Dole, France, 24
drugs, 7, 64–66

Ebola, 6, 13, 87
economics, impact of diseases on, 6, 79–82
ecosystem, 8
emerging infectious diseases, 89–90. *See
    also* infectious diseases
encephalitis, 27
endotracheal intubation, 39
enveloped virus, 31
epidemic, 19
epithelial cells, 41

Federal Quarantine Legislation, 47
fibrogranulative tissue, 41
Flemming, Alexander, 64–65
Foshan, China, 17
French Hospital (Hanoi, Vietnam), 8–9
de Freudenreich, E., 64

Geneva, Switzerland, 18
genome, 35
geographical region, 8
germs, 64
germ theory and disease, 26
global epidemics, 90–94
gloves, 53, 91
glycyrrhizin, 67
GNP. *See* Gross National Product
Gross National Product (GNP), 82
Guangdong Province, China
    first human cases of SARS, 15, 17, 19,
        35–36, 89
    spread of SARS, 14
    travel advisory, 93
Guangzhou, China, 17
The Guardian, 23

H5N1. *See* avian influenza A
hand washing, 48, 91
Hanoi, Vietnam, 10, 18, 20
HCoVs (human coronaviruses), 32
health, defined, 18
health alert, 20, 94
health care personnel, 52, 91
Hebei Province, China, 101
helical virus, 31
hemolytic anemia, 66
herbal remedies, 67, 68
HIV, 87
Hong Kong
    control and management of SARS, 92,
        94
    health alert, 20
    SARS research, 35
    spread of SARS, 8–9, 17, 45
    travel advisory, 49, 93
    treatment of SARS, 68
Honolulu, Hawaii, 47
host, 14, 26, 28

icosahedral virus, 30
immune system, 29–30, 50
immunoglobulins, 67–68
immunomodulatory properties, 66
incidence of infection, 31
incubation period, 42
index case, 17
infection, defined, 23
infectious disease, 13–15, 26, 87–90
inflammatory response, 41
influenza, 27
innate immune system, 41
Inner Mongolia, 101
inoculum, 42
in polio, 7
interferon, 29, 41, 67–68
intracellular parasites. *See* virus
intubation, 91
isolation, 21, 62, 68, 73–74

Jenner, Edward, 25, 71
job losses, 82

Killer Bug. *See* SARS
Koch, Robert, 26

Koch's postulates, 26, 34, 100
Kwok-Yung, Yuen, 92

laboratory tests, 50
leprosy, 6
lessons learned from SARS outbreak, 95–96
leucopenia, 58
Los Angeles, California, 47
lungs, 43
lymphatic filariasis, 6
lymphocytes. *See* blood cells, white
lymphopenia, 58

macrophages, 30
malaria, 6, 7, 87
management of SARS. *See* SARS,
    management of
Manila, Philippines, 19
masked palm civet. *See* civet
masks. *See* surgical masks
Marburg hemorrhagic fevers, 6
media coverage, 82–83
medications. *See* drugs
Metropole Hotel (Hong Kong), 8–9, 17, 18
Miami, Florida, 47
microorganism, 23–26
mosquito, 8

N95 respirator, 54
National Institutes of Health (NIH), 72
National Microbiology Laboratory
    (Canada), 34
nebulizer, 44, 91
necrosis, 41
New Delhi, India, 19
New York City, New York, 47
NIH. *See* National Institutes of Health
nosocomial, 46
nucleocapsid, 36

onchocerciais, 6
open reading frames (ORFs), 36
oral-fecal transmission, 42
ORFs. *See* open reading frames

Pagnuma larvata. *See* civet
Pasteur, Louis, 24–25, 64
pathogenesis, 40
pathogens, 21

PCR. *See* polymerase chain reaction
pebrine, 25
Peiris, Malik, 34
penicillin, 65
Penicillium, 64
peplomers, 31
Philippines, 19, 45
pneumococcal pneumonia, 7
pneumonia. *See* atypical pneumonia
polio, 6
polymerase chain reaction (PCR), 55, 93, 95
prevention. *See* SARS, prevention of
probable case, 60–61
proteases, 68
Pseudomonas aeruginosa, 41
public health measures, 73–78
Public Health Service, 76
public panic, 82–83
pulmonary fibrosis, 43

quarantine, 21, 22, 46–48, 52, 63–64, 91,
    92, 95, 100
Queens, New York, 89

rabies, 25, 27
raccoon dog, 54
RBD. *See* receptor-binding domain
receptor-binding domain (RBD), 69
re-emerging infections, 6, 7
replicase, 36
respiratory distress, 43
respiratory infections, 6
ribonucleic acid. *See* RNA
risk factors, 51–55
RNA (ribonucleic acid), 27, 28, 31, 36
Royal Society (London), 96

safety gear, 53. *See also* gloves; surgical masks
Salk, Jonas, 76
San Francisco, California, 47
SARS. *See* severe acute respiratory syndrome
SARS-CoV. *See* SARS
Seattle, Washington, 47
sensitivity, 56
severe acute respiratory syndrome (SARS), 6
    animal origins, 35–36
    case definition, 60–61, 94
    cause of, 34–35
    classification categories, 60

containment, 21
controlling, 83–84, 91
described, 13–15, 40–41
diagnosis of, 46–48, 50–51, 52, 58–60, 85
economic significance of, 79–82, 84
efforts to stop, 84–86
exposure to, 42, 52
future responses, 95–97
global epidemic, 8–21
health crisis, 48
identifying, 90–91
immune system, 29–30
impact of, 79–86
lessons learned, 87–98
management of, 50–51, 57, 62
managing, 91
mortality rates, 8, 20–21
origins and spread of, 15–20
preventative measures, 48
prevention of, 73–78
psychological impact, 83
retrospective examination of, 93–95
SARS-associated coronavirus
    (SARS-CoV), 31–33
significance of, 79–86
study of, 34
symptoms, 39–40, 42–44
transmission of, 37, 39–40, 44–46, 75–77,
    91
treatment of, 62–72
viral infections, 22–38
virus, 22–38
Singapore
economic and political impact of SARS, 79
Ministry of Health, 52
spread of SARS, 18–19, 46
smallpox, 7, 19, 71
sputum induction, 39
squamous metaplasia, 41
Staphylococcus bacteria, 64–65
subpleural proliferation, 41
superspreading, 45–46, 100
surgical masks, 53, 54, 63, 80, 91
suspected case, 60

T cells, 30
Taipei, 79, 101
Taiwan, 49, 90
testing for SARS, 55–56, 61

thrombocytopenia, 58
TIME magazine, 23
Toronto, Canada
case cluster, 34
SARS cluster in hospital, 19
SARS transmission, 18, 45
tourism, impact of SARS on, 13
travel advisory, 49, 93
tourism. *See* travel and SARS
transaminase, 66
travel and SARS
effects on, 79–82
travel advisory, 15, 49, 93–94
travel restrictions, 81
treatment, 68–69
tuberculosis, 6, 7, 26, 87

University of Hong Kong, 34
University of Lille, 24
Urbani, Carlo, 9, 43
USDA. *See* U.S. Department of Agriculture
U.S. Department of Agriculture (USDA), 47

vaccines, 25, 69–72, 95, 102
variant of Creutzfeldt-Jakob disease
    (vCJD), 6
variolation, 71
vCJD. *See* variant of Creutzfeldt-Jakob
    disease
vector, 8, 39
Venice, Italy, 47
Vero cell, 32
Vietnam, 8–9, 8–9, 10, 18, 20
control and management of SARS, 94
SARS transmission, 93
travel advisory, 49
viral load, 42
viral shredding, 46
virion, 36
virus, 13, 27
cause infection and, 28–29
described, 26–27
hosts and, 27
replication, 27
types of, 30–31

Wall Street Journal, 97
Washington, D.C., 19
West Nile virus, 89

WHO. *See* World Health Organization
World Health Assembly, 18, 97
World Health Organization (WHO), 9, 10
  case definition of SARS, 94
  control and management of SARS, 13,
    16, 83
  described, 18–19
  diagnosis guidelines, 85
  disease outbreak information, 91
  health alert, 20
  lessons learned from SARS outbreak,
    95–96
  naming of SARS virus, 34
  travel advisory, 15, 49, 93
  Web sites, 81
World Travel and Tourism Council, 82

zoonosis, 95

About the Author

Joaquima Serradell graduated with a degree in clinical pharmacy from the University of Barcelona, Spain. She also holds both a Master of Public Health and a Ph.D. in Social and Administrative Pharmacy from the University of Minnesota.

She completed a postdoctoral research fellowship at the United States Pharmacopeia and has taught and conducted research at the Philadelphia College of Pharmacy and at the Department of Medicine of the University of Pennsylvania. She is currently a consultant in the fields of pharmacoepidemiology and international aspects of health-care delivery. She has written numerous articles and book chapters on the behavioral, epidemiological, and economic aspects of drug use.

About the Consulting Editor

Hilary Babcock, M.D., M.P.H., is an Assistant Professor of Medicine at Washington University School of Medicine at Washington University School of Medicine and the Medical Director of Occupational Health for Barnes-Jewish Hospital and St. Louis Children's Hospital. She received her undergraduate degree from Brown University and her M.D. from the University of Texas Southwestern Medical Center at Dallas. After completing her residency, chief residency, and Infectious Disease fellowship at Barnes-Jewish Hospital, she joined the faculty of the Infectious Disease division. She completed an M.P.H. in Public Health from St. Louis University School of Public Health in 2006. She has lectured, taught, and written extensively about infectious diseases, their treatment, and their prevention. She is a member of numerous medical associations and is board certified in infectious disease. She lives in St. Louis, Missouri.